INDIE AUTHOR MAGAZINE

HELLO AND WELCOME!

I'm Indie Annie, and I'm thrilled you're reading this gorgeous full-color version of IAM. Did you know that you can also access all the information, education, and inspiration in our app? It's available on both the iOS App Store and Google Play. And for those that prefer to listen to me read articles, you can pop over to Spotify or our website. Happy Reading!

X

IndieAuthorMagazine.com

ORGANIC TRAFFIC

18
ORGANIZING CHAOS
Beyond The 2023 Author's Planner, Audrey Hughey Helps Others Plan for the Future

28
A PEEK BEHIND THE TABLE
How to Prepare for Your First Signing Event as an Author

34
THE DOS AND DON'TS OF CREATING YOUR READER MAGNET

40
#UNFILTERED
What Authors Say Online Matters to Their Readers, So How Much Should You Be Sharing on Social Media?

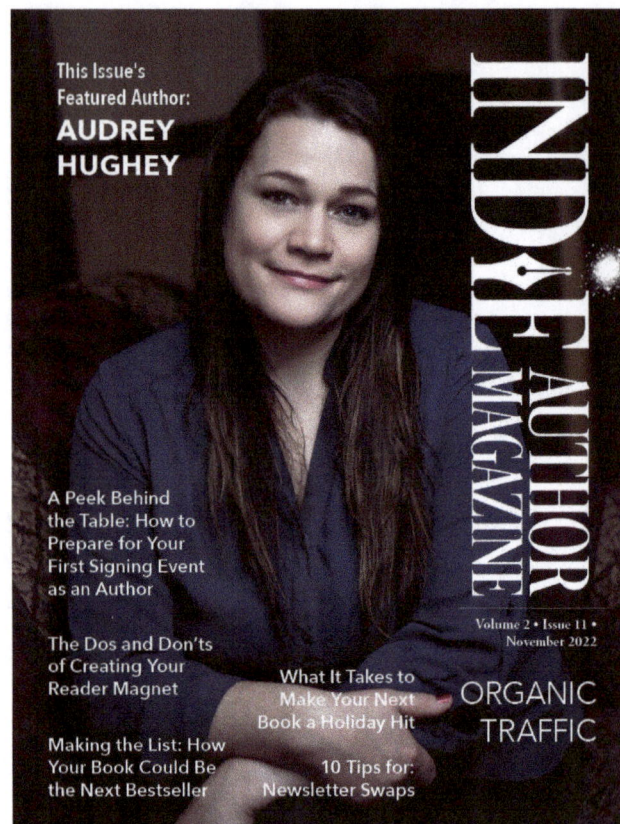

This Issue's Featured Author: AUDREY HUGHEY

INDIE AUTHOR MAGAZINE

A Peek Behind the Table: How to Prepare for Your First Signing Event as an Author

The Dos and Don'ts of Creating Your Reader Magnet

What It Takes to Make Your Next Book a Holiday Hit

Making the List: How Your Book Could Be the Next Bestseller

10 Tips for: Newsletter Swaps

Volume 2 • Issue 11 • November 2022

ORGANIC TRAFFIC

ON THE COVER

INDiE
AUTHOR MAGAZINE

PUBLISHER
Chelle Honiker

CREATIVE DIRECTOR
Alice Briggs

EDITOR IN CHIEF
Nicole Schroeder

COPY EDITOR
Lisa Thompson

WRITERS
Angela Archer
Elaine Bateman
Patricia Carr
Bradley Charbonneau
Laurel Decher
Fatima Fayez
Gill Fernley
Greg Fishbone
Belinda Griffin
Chrishaun Keller-Hanna
Jac Harmon
Marion Hermannsen

WRITERS
Kasia Lasinska
Megan Linski-Fox
Bre Lockhart
Sìne Màiri MacDougall
Angie Martin
Merri Maywether
Susan Odev
Jenn Mitchell
Clare Sager
Nicole Schroeder
Emilia Zeeland

PUBLISHER
Athenia Creative
6820 Apus Dr.
Sparks, NV, 89436 USA
775.298.1925

ISSN 2768-7880 (online)–ISSN 2768-7872 (print)

From the Publisher

Recently I had the pleasure of interviewing potential new contributors for *Indie Author Magazine*. Thirty-four brave souls stepped forward for consideration and a thirty-minute Zoom interview. Rather than feeling like thirty-four business meetings, it was instead a delight to meet some of the smartest, most interesting writers in our field. It was a personal reminder of our history and mission, and it reinforced my enthusiasm for our future. Here are some of the things I realized.

OUR READERSHIP IS TRULY GLOBAL.

I spoke with writers from South Africa, Nigeria, the United Kingdom, the United States, India, Ireland, Canada, Georgia, and Australia. They shared their love of writing and connecting with their readers. I met community leaders, poet laureates, university professors, and self-described "regular moms" who juggle writing and homeschooling. Having been that mom many moons ago, I can attest there is nothing "regular" about that. It's like being a lion tamer in a circus—and the big top is on fire. Each story was extraordinary.

WE HAVE AN EXCEPTIONAL ORIGIN STORY AND MISSION.

On each call, I recapped how we started and distilled nearly two years' worth of work into a thirty-second elevator pitch. And each time it reminded me of how hard this team has worked to help our community. Every article was born of a question, and we've done our best to provide a thoughtful, well-researched answer. Our mission is clear, and it's being fulfilled with every issue.

WE HAVE A BRIGHT FUTURE.

I can't wait to see the ideas this group of new authors will bring to the magazine in the coming months. We're hard at work making room for expanded sections and more trusted voices who will share ideas with you on a broad array of subjects. I'm confident they'll bring fresh perspectives and fresh energy, and that will make us even better in the future.

To Your Success,
Chelle
Chelle Honiker, Publisher & Co-Founder
Indie Author Magazine, Indie Author Tools, Author Tech Summit

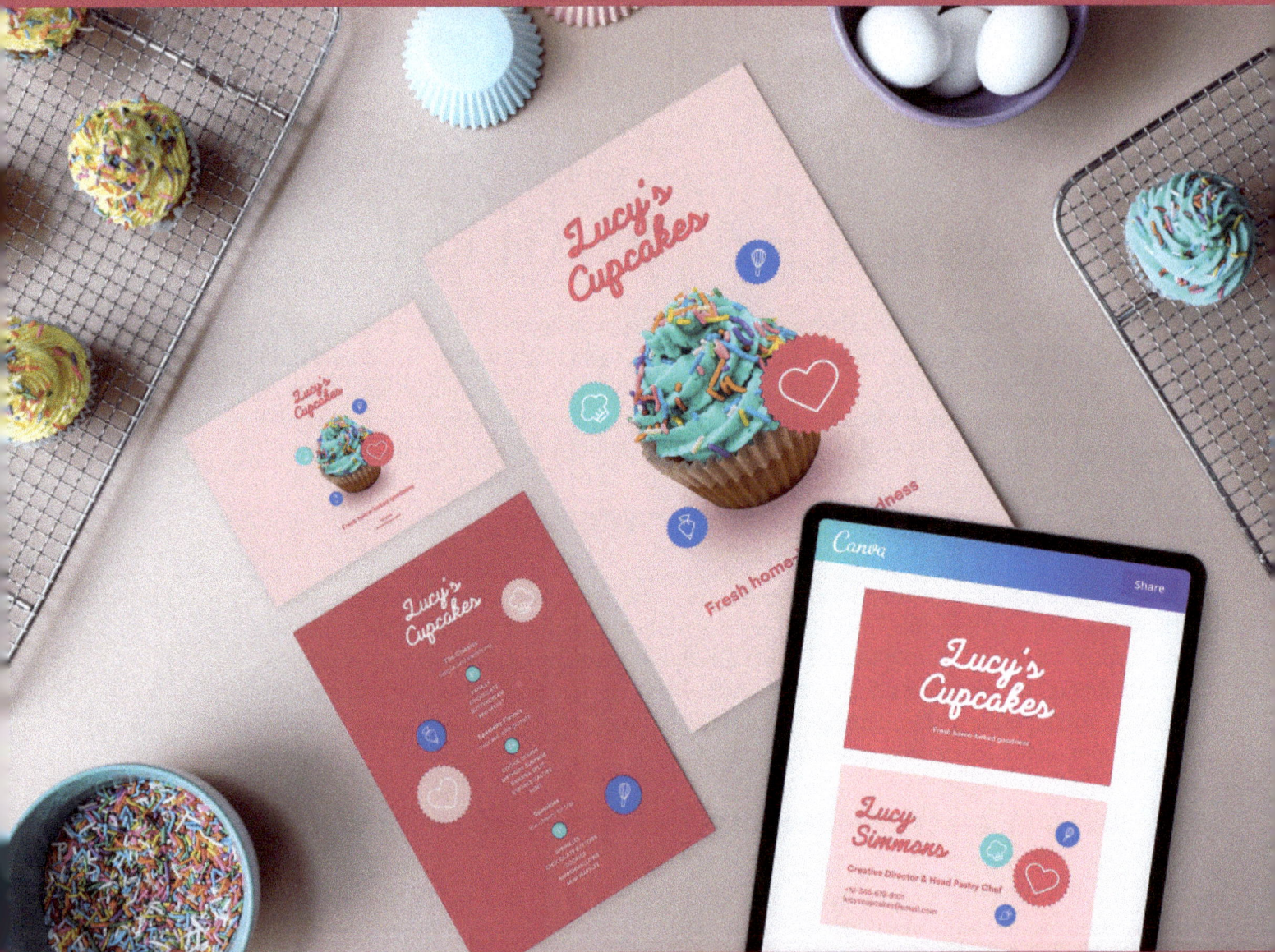

Design like a Pro for free

From the Editor in Chief

In American Sign Language, to sign the word "friend," you hook your two pointer fingers together, then flip both hands over and repeat the action. When I was learning sign language in college, the website we used as a reference said to imagine your fingers were hugging. Instead, I like to think of things connecting.

With National Novel Writing Month (NaNoWriMo), a flood of end-of-the-year releases and launch parties, and, of course, 20Books Vegas, there's undeniably a lot to juggle in November—and that's without worrying about the start of the holiday season. If you're anything like me, in a month that can be arguably one of the busiest in our industry, you'll likely be burning a candle at both ends to make everything fit into your schedule. And eventually, you'll start to run out of wick.

But it's in those moments when I find my candle growing dimmer that I think back to the sign for "friend." These events are all important to our careers as individual authors, sure. But they're also some of the best opportunities we have to make connections with one another. Your local NaNoWriMo group might become some of your loudest cheerleaders, like they were for Audrey Hughey, this month's featured author. That launch party you host could introduce a host of new readers to your work—and if you need ideas, check out Angie Martin's feature on how to prepare for your first author signing event. And this year's 20Books Vegas conference might just bring you closer to other authors and publishing professionals who will help your career soar to new heights.

To create friends, you first have to form connections. And although this month asks a lot of us, it gives us plenty of those opportunities in return. We'll replenish our candles next month—for now, let's use them to find new people, exchange stories, and connect.

Nicole Schroeder
Editor in Chief
Indie Author Magazine

The Power of In-Person Author Conferences

We have 20Books Vegas 2022 coming up soon, which means it's time for a quick refresher on the value of in-person conferences.

Motivation and positive vibes. Authors are happiest when they are around other authors. It brings most of us out of our shells because we find people with whom we don't have to make small talk. We find our tribe.

And that's the most important part of all. Most conferences have a social media surge prior to the show. Find that person who you can relate to, a person who writes in your genre and is maybe at the same place in their author journey. Meet up with them at check-in, and you'll find that it's a lot easier when you're going through the unknown with a friend, even if they were a stranger until moments before.

It's not about an introvert becoming an extrovert. It's about an introvert tapping into what makes them who they are—the ability to focus on things that are important to them. Extroverts will find plenty of people who could use a friend. Look for them, but don't overwhelm them. Be at ease. Extroverts will seem like they are thriving, but they also have the challenge of too many people. Will they get anything substantive out of the conversations? They have to also work outside of their norm to get the most from a show.

Don't be alone in a crowd. When you realize that you're surrounded by people who are just like you, it will take the edge off, but only if you open your mind. There will be noise, but that's because people are excited to see old friends and new. Wear earplugs until you find someone you've met, even if only online. Give yourself power over your environment.

And have a plan. Plan your session attendance based on your business needs. See the guest speakers; talk to them to fill in gaps in your foundation. Get better at craft. Get better at ads. Get better at blurbs. Hire a great cover artist. There are so many opportunities at in-person events that will enable you to take your business to the next level.

And that's why you invest money for in-person events. You are investing in yourself. Fear the failure of not getting your business off the ground, but don't be afraid of talking with the people who can help you prevent that.

Consider at least one in-person author conference and go. Learn and grow. Build a strong business, and free yourself. ■

Craig Martelle

Dear Indie Annie,

I was so excited when I started my series, and now I feel like I might lose the will to live if I have to write any more. The problem is that I have a big fan base and they are clamoring for the next book. Writing is my sole source of income, so I need to continue to write what the fans love. How do I fall back in love with my characters and series?

Out of Love in Obura

DEAR OUT OF LOVE,

I'm sorry, that moniker is too long. I'm going to call you Obura. Yes, that's better. Obura sounds like an excellent name for a character. You know, sometimes my mind and fingers wander and, so inspired, I started to create a character sketch for a female warrior called Obura.

It haunted me like it was familiar, somehow, so I hit the source of all truth: Google.

And there was Obara Sands, a character from the legendary series that is *Game of Thrones*. I accept the reason I found Obara was because I mistyped Obura, but it was a happy coincidence because it got me thinking about the answer to your question.

George R. R. Martin.

That's the answer—or, rather, he is.

Admittedly, this answer is almost as cryptic as the answer to the meaning of life in Douglas Adams's *The Hitchhiker's Guide to the Galaxy*, and though I'm not going to spoil it for you in case you have yet to read this humorous masterpiece, please stick with me, my dear Obura, because I will reveal all.

Whether you like Epic Fantasy, you would have to have been living in a cave on an isolated island in the middle of the Indian Ocean with no Wi-Fi connection to have not heard about the success of *Game of Thrones*. This incredibly popular TV series was based on Martin's book series *A Song of Ice and Fire*. Now, I could fill up this letter giving you the timeline of Martin's books, but you can check it out on Wikipedia. The gist of it is that he started writing his first book in 1991. It was finally published in 1996 and was meant to be part of a trilogy. That morphed into a planned seven-volume set. Book five, *A Dance with Dragons*, came out in 2011—a full six years after book four—and we are all still eagerly awaiting the last two books.

George R. R. Martin is now in his seventies, and maybe fans will remain disappointed. However, by scouring through articles, interviews, and even Martin's own blog—cheekily named "Not a Blog"—we can pick out Martin's writing process. He writes from

Need help from your favorite Indie Aunt?
Ask Dear Indie Annie a question at
IndieAnnie@indieauthormagazine.com

twenty different points of view and will only write on days when he has nothing else but writing to do. That's a lot of characters to stay engaged with, but it still takes phenomenal writing endurance to stay interested in your story and the people who inhabit it for that long.

You state that the income from your books is your only source of income, so it seems to me that you have four options:

1. Become as successful as Mr. Martin so that you lock yourself in a log cabin and write for six-plus years on the next book in your series. He has, after all, demonstrated that your fans will keep buying and will wait if they love what you do.
2. Give up writing and get a proper job. The suffering of the mind-numbing nine-to-five will make your boring characters appear much more attractive.
3. Suck it up, and remember this is a business. Yes, it's a creative business and you need to reengage with your muse somehow, but at the end of the day, this is a job, and sometimes you have to do stuff at work that is mundane and kills you slowly on the inside.
4. Ignore the fans, write a fresh series, and hope they follow you on your next adventure with no ill feeling. (Have you watched or read Stephen King's *Misery*?)

What you have to ask yourself, my dear Obura, is which of these options feels most palatable?

Alternatively, you could try falling back in love again with your series. Take your characters on a date. Wine and dine them. Have fun with them. Put them in a new situation—maybe they could go on a vacation or meet someone new. Could they nip across to a spin-off series for a bit of extracurricular fun?

Why don't you try sitting down with them over a coffee and get reacquainted? They will have changed; we all do. Perhaps they need an opportunity to grow. If you really can't stand them anymore, torture them a little. Throw them a massive curveball. Relocate them. Kill one of them off. Send them off to work abroad. What I beg of you is not to just send them upstairs in one scene for them never to be heard of again. They have served you well and deserve better than that. Still not engaged? You could always write away everything that has happened to them in the past as a dream.

Whatever you do, make it fun. Enjoy it, and your fans will too.

Happy writing,
Indie Annie

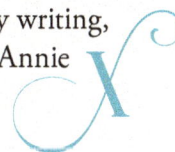

10 TIPS FOR
NEWSLETTER SWAPS

Roughly six years ago, a well-known Contemporary Romance author organized a book promotion. She posted the invite to participate in a Facebook group and opened it up to all authors, writing that she remembered her beginnings in the author world and that nobody would be excluded because their mailing lists were too small. Those who wanted to take part added their book for free, and once it kicked off, every participating author shared the promotion with their audience.

At the time I joined, my mailing list size was zero. The organizing author assured me that didn't matter.

In the end, over two hundred authors contributed to the promotion and shared one another's books with their readers. Only one book had a cover sans a man's chest—mine. What's the word for beyond embarrassed? I thought for sure the Romance reader and author community would laugh me into oblivion.

But that didn't happen.

There were wins: I ended up with two thousand readers on my list. Some of my staunchest supporters came from that swap. There were uh-ohs: It took years for the Amazon algorithm to straighten out my books' "also bought" categories. And although I ultimately lost a majority of those two thousand readers when both of us realized that our author-reader relationship wasn't a good fit, I learned a lot about the importance of newsletter swaps.

Exchanging information with an author in order to share your books with each another's newsletters is a great way to put your work in front of new audiences and increase sales, but only when done correctly. To help you avoid my mistakes, and hopefully repeat the wins, we've compiled a list of ten tips for cementing the perfect newsletter swap—one that will ensure you get the right reader's eyes on your books.

① FIND AUTHORS WILLING TO SHARE YOUR BOOK

Thanks to the widespread philosophy that all indies benefit when we help one another, there are a variety of ways to find people who will swap newsletters. Beyond reaching out to authors individually, communities found through Amazon's KBoards, genre-focused Facebook groups, and newsletter swap sites can all help authors connect with others who are looking to form newsletter swaps.

The most common three swap sites are Prolific Works, BookFunnel, and Story Origin, but there are more out there. When you join these sites, you'll create a profile and add the details about the book you want others to share. Authors will then post either a promotion or a direct swap. A promotion is a pool of authors sending readers to a landing page, where they will decide which books tap into their interest. A direct swap is when an author mentions your book with links to the sales page. In other words, both of you will send a newsletter with a mention of each other's books.

Pro Tip: Do not join KBoards or a genre group just to find people for a newsletter swap. The owners of these groups create them to make space for discussions that help the community, and you don't want to take advantage of others without contributing something in return. Instead, engage with others authentically. In time, established authors will post that they are looking for swaps, or the group administrator will create a post for people to find others to swap with. In the comments, you'll find people who can help get the word out about your book.

② STAY IN YOUR LANE

The idea of getting your book in front of potentially thousands of readers' eyes seems exciting, but if they are the wrong readers, it is an exercise in futility. Look for authors who write in the same genre and niche you do before you decide whether their books are good candidates for a swap. Remember, your audience has expectations. When they are hearing from someone known for Science Fiction and who delivers stories with aliens and weapons, they might not care about a character who uses essences and can kill magical beings with one dagger slice. They'll be disappointed, then you'll be disappointed.

③ DO YOUR RESEARCH

Authors initiating a swap often have their cover, tagline, and blurb listed with the rest of their information. Samples of the book are available on most e-book retailers, so before you offer to swap with them, read a couple of pages to see if the author is a good fit. Does their story entice you to delve deeper into the book? Are there typos? Remember, your readers trust your word. If they check out what you share and encounter several stories that aren't up to their standards, they might lose trust in your recommendations.

④ BE HONEST ABOUT WHAT YOU HAVE

I've been there. We've all been there. Everyone's list size must start somewhere, so if you don't have a large list, just say so. What is your social media reach? Perhaps you don't have subscribers, but you have an author page on Facebook or an active blog with regular readership. If you don't have a large list, or even a list at all, think of ways you can contribute to helping someone reach more readers. If you can reach an audience that another author can't in order to get word out about their book, you can still contribute meaningfully to a swap. Having a small newsletter reach likely won't ruin your chances of organizing a successful swap with an author, but being dishonest about your list size certainly will.

(5) DECIDE A PURPOSE FOR YOUR SWAP

Newsletters are used for a variety of purposes. Are you trying to grow your mailing list, promote a launch, or give a release some traction? Decide why you'd like to swap, and explain that to the person you are swapping with. This will help the other author determine if what you're presenting will fit in with what they're sharing with their readers.

(6) FOLLOW THROUGH WITH YOUR COMMITMENT

This is simple etiquette. Treat others the way you want to be treated. If you tell an author you're going to share their work with readers but change your mind, you have broken an agreement and lost trust with that author—and possibly many others. Of course, unforeseen events that prohibit writing happen. If there's an emergency or other issue that arises that prevents you from posting the swap when you originally promised, communicate this with the other author as soon as possible to reschedule to a time when you can follow through with the commitment.

(7) SWAP WITH YOUR READERS IN MIND

A newsletter is a written conversation with your readers; if they wanted a list of books, they'd sign up for a service that promises them that. Readers signed up for your newsletter because they want to hear from you, so even when sharing newsletter swaps, continue with the practice. Many authors prefer to write their normal correspondence at the top. Then, at the bottom, they'll share the other author's books under a clear and easily recognizable heading. Just be sure your readers know to keep scrolling once your message is done. Consider teasing the swap in your letter or posing a question in the subject line, then promising to answer at the bottom of the newsletter.

(8) SWAP WITH OTHER AUTHORS IN MIND

When another author agrees to swap with you, share your book cover, tagline, blurb, and the link to your sales page. Having to search for information is a time drag. If you don't offer what your swap partners need, they might not be able to provide their readers enough information to find your books or take any interest in your stories. They're not being mean; it's a way of conserving time so they can focus on their own businesses. However, if you put all your information clearly in front of them, your swap partners will be able to share most, if not all, the information their readers need to decide whether your book is a good fit.

Pro Tip: Depending on how much room they have in their newsletter, your swap partner may still only have room to use the image, tagline, and link to your story, even if you've provided them more information. These are the primary details you should expect to see in a swap, so don't be upset if they've left off something you sent in addition—it will still be plenty for their readers to find you. But it's yet another reason to make sure your cover can hold its own and sell your story well.

9 STICK TO YOUR SCHEDULE

There isn't a prescribed time to send out newsletters with swaps. However, if you make a commitment to your readers on the frequency with which you'll send them recommendations, follow through with it. This sets the bar for your readers' expectations and proves your reliability to readers and other authors.

10 TRACK AND MEASURE RESULTS

If you're swapping with several other authors, you'll want to have a way to measure success and attribute it to the right campaign. Add a simple tracking code to your website link, and track clicks in Google Analytics using a UTM code that includes the name of the campaign.

Pro Tip: Not sure how UTM codes work? Watch the video primer on our YouTube channel.

The source and medium can be the same for each link, with just the campaign name changing depending on the author you're swapping with. It's a free-form field that passes the information over to Google. That way, when you look in Google Analytics, you'll see the clicks registered under the Source/Medium report. If you're not using Google Analytics to measure traffic to your website, you can also use a free link shortener like https://bitly.com to create a short link for each author you swap with.

Acquisition						
Overview	☐	1.	(direct) / (none)	(not set)	**51**	(30.91%)
▼ All Traffic	☐	2.	sendinblue / email	Friday- Reedsy Free Replay Now Open	**34**	(20.61%)
Channels	☐	3.	sendinblue / email	Thursday Reminder- Reedsy Replay	**29**	(17.58%)
Treemaps	☐	4.	m.facebook.com / referral	(not set)	**14**	(8.48%)
Source/Medium	☐	5.	sendinblue / email	Call For Presenters	**11**	(6.67%)
Referrals	☐	6.	l.facebook.com / referral	(not set)	**8**	(4.85%)

Whether it's your first or your fiftieth newsletter swap, it's important to take steps to ensure the process is organized and will benefit you, your swap partner, and your readers. By putting in the effort now, you'll have the opportunity to not only sell more books; you'll also be able to build relationships that will pay back dividends for years to come. ■

Merri Maywether

Organizing Chaos

BEYOND THE 2023 AUTHOR'S PLANNER, AUDREY HUGHEY HELPS OTHERS PLAN FOR THE FUTURE

When Audrey Hughey heard about a business planner created by female entrepreneur Carrie Green in 2017, she was hooked. The problem: As it was the first year they were being printed, and with the cost of shipping and exchange rates, Audrey wasn't able to save up enough to buy one before they were out of stock. But the missed opportunity gave her an idea. "I had tried so many planners before, and … no matter how many pretty planners with pretty covers I bought, none of them hit the spot for what I needed in my life," she says. "I needed something that told me on every page that writing is a core, central piece of my life." So, she thought, why not create a planner of her own?

At the time, Audrey was six weeks away from the end of the year and knee-deep in a draft for National Novel Writing Month, or NaNoWriMo. But that didn't faze her. With printing schedules, she knew she'd need to have the project finished and ready to ship before the first of the year. So she got to work.

For several days, she didn't sleep or see much of her family. She ate most meals bent over her keyboard as she tried to piece everything together before her deadline. Two weeks later, however, the first proof was finished. By the first part of December, after she'd completed another round of revisions, she was holding the printed proof of the 2018 Author's Journal in her hands.

Five years later, as an indie author herself and the founder of the Author Transformation Alliance (ATA), Audrey's planners are

far from her only endeavor. Audrey says she likes to use the title "authorpreneur" to describe her work—"but I don't want to be too cliche."

"I really dabble in a lot of things," she says. "I'm always exploring what I love and my purpose." Now, with the seventh iteration of her author planner published in October and as she prepares for a major rebrand of her business this month, it seems the author and creator has found that purpose.

"I can't quite put my finger on it—she has a knack for understanding what writers need," says author P. A. Duncan. And whether those authors connect with her through her planners, the sprint groups she's organized, or the conferences and podcasts where she's presented, most end up knowing her best for the positivity and support she offers them.

ONE WOMAN, MANY HATS

Audrey's author business would be plenty to juggle on its own, but it isn't the only thing keeping her busy. Outside of the writing world, she's also a mom of five children, her oldest a twenty-three-year-old and her youngest having turned a year old in September. As expected, the role comes with its own host of responsibilities—even those as unusual as needing to rescue the family's missing cat in the middle of our interview.

With motherhood as her full-time job, Audrey says she fits writing into her schedule a few spare moments at a time. She wakes up to write sometime between when her husband gets up at 3 a.m. and when she wakes up her children at 6:30 a.m., then snags a bit more time once the kids are at school and the baby is settled for the morning. She says she prefers to tackle her to-do list in batches, focusing largely on a single project until it's complete. "For some people, they want that steady consistency, doing the same thing every day. But for me, life doesn't work with that, especially because I have so many kids going through so many different stages."

As for where she writes? These days, most of Audrey's writing takes place at home, but last year, when she was still pregnant, she often enjoyed doing her work at Starbucks. "That is my happy place to go and write and get the words in," she says.

Even with all the organization it takes for her to put words down, the words themselves can sometimes be a surprise. The woman creating the planners isn't always a planner herself, at least with her story worlds. And though her current work in progress is fully outlined, when she isn't on deadline, she enjoys "pantsing"—a term adopted by NaNoWriMo participants that refers to writing by the seat of one's pants—her way to a finished draft.

A.K. HUGHEY

HUNTING DARKNESS

SMALL TOWN SECRETS

It isn't just her plotting styles that vary. "I really want to explore what I love, what I enjoy, and just write stories that call to me," Audrey says. Contrary to how many indie authors find success, she writes in a variety of genres, some under the same pen name. She admits she has a penchant for buying premade covers, and several ideas have come from the collection she's amassed or ideas she's let percolate until she feels she can do them justice. Her author brand isn't built around a particular genre or target audience, and that is purposeful.

"I think that we shouldn't take for granted that we're in an age where we can explore what we want to write as indie authors, and we're not boxed into some requirements by a publisher about what they will and won't accept based on what they think is marketable," she says. "I just can't imagine a life spent coloring in the lines when we might be interested in something just a little out of bounds."

THE ROAD TO A WRITING CAREER

Audrey's preference for a variety of genres isn't all that surprising, given how she grew up. With a dad who read Michael Crichton and Stephen King and a mom who added Piers Anthony and Anne McCaffrey to the shelves, her family's home library offered plenty to choose from. But as much as she loved reading the stories, Audrey also loved creating them.

As a child, she would whisper stories to her horses while on trail rides and pen Westerns and Fantasies as soon as she could write. "I think I just have it in my blood," she says. Most of her family enjoys either music or storytelling, and today, several of her family members—her cousins Robert E. Keller and John Keller, her grandmother Mary B. Knapp, and her great aunt Kathy Mendoza, among others—are authors and award-winning writers themselves.

As she got older, Audrey's love for stories remained, though her own interests grew to include ancient history and Greek mythology—tales she credits with helping open her mind to other cultures. That cultural awareness would serve her well when she entered the military in 2003. Over the next fourteen years, she spent time in both Germany and Afghanistan, including in combat zones.

For a while, she says, her books took a back seat to the rest of her life. But her experiences during those years taught her other important lessons, she says. "Spending enough time in combat zones—for many people, I think you come out of it with a different perspective about what's worth freaking out over." The obstacles she faces today—be it a surgery, a vacation gone awry, or a missing cat—can be overcome; she just has to stay calm and adapt. Eventually, when she was stationed in Kandahar, Afghanistan, as a contractor in 2012, her schedule opened up enough for her to write again in the mornings. And by the time she'd moved back to West Virginia and discovered her local NaNoWriMo group a couple of years later, it had become more than a pastime. When she published her first book in 2019, she says, she realized it had become "this piece of my life that I couldn't let go anymore."

But why self-publishing? Audrey never really considered traditional publishing for her books—even with her military background, she jokes she has a tendency to "question 'authority.'" Where she had seen traditional publishing turn away a friend's manuscript because the female main character didn't cry enough, independent publishing offered Audrey a chance to control her own stories and shift the narrative.

"It never made sense to me. … How can we change literature if we keep being wrapped into these boundaries that are created just for the sake of predicted marketability?" she says. "(With self-publishing,) I don't have to wait for someone to give me the green light to write my own characters and my own stories."

SHARING THE WISDOM

As time has gone on, more projects have found their way into Audrey's world. In February 2017, she founded the ATA, a place for writers to share resources and view courses related to the business side of publishing. A few months later, in November of the same year, the Author's Planner was born. For Audrey, the tools and resources are a way to give back to the indie author community. But they've also helped support many authors as they've worked to grow their careers.

"It's one thing to say, 'I want to write a book,' or 'I want to be a six-figure author,'" says Epic Fantasy and Paranormal author Emily Burch Harris, a member

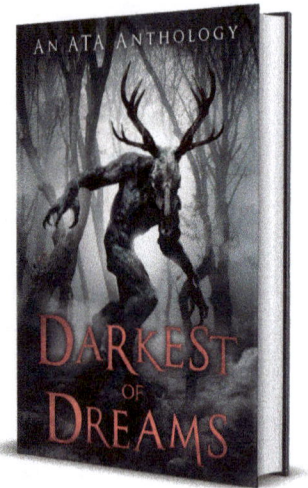

of ATA. "It's another thing to actually sit down with someone who knows how to put that into a scalable action plan."

Audrey says the messages she's received about how her work has helped people have become some of the most rewarding memories she has from her career. Publishing can be a hard road, she continues, but it shouldn't be one authors feel they have to travel alone. "If I can help somebody in any way, whether through planning or time management or just an encouraging word, feel better about where they are and where they're going, then I should be doing that."

WHAT'S NEXT

In Audrey's case, the answer to where she's going is the same as it is for many other indie authors later this month, as she's set to attend this year's 20Books Vegas conference November 14–18. But even before that, she'll have plenty of opportunities to fill her planner's pages. The 2023 Author's Planner launched mid-October, and her author support business is set to undergo a major rebrand before the start of this year's conference. After that, she'll take a break, she says, to spend time with family, reflect on what she's accomplished, and start looking ahead to next year.

As for the authors who are ready to do the same, remember that "it's not about planning out a day and having it happen perfectly because that is not life," she says. "Life does not happen perfectly." Instead, the process is about finding goals that you truly want to reach and making strides toward them a little at a time. And it can be as easy as the thought exercise in the front of her planners.

"Think about December 31 of the coming year," she says. "It's New Year's Eve, and you're celebrating. Your loved one—the person that you would spend that night with that is most important to you—they ask you, 'What are you most proud of accomplishing this year?' What is that one thing that you would be most proud … to accomplish in 2023? Think about that. Get super clear on that, and then create your goals for the coming year." ■

Nicole Schroeder

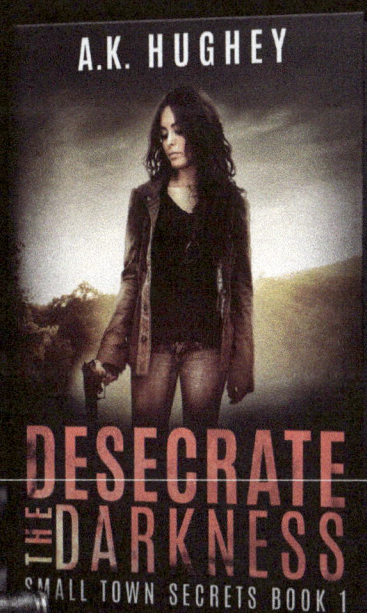

All Work, But Plenty of Play Too

THE 2022 NINC CONFERENCE IN REVIEW

Books on the beach sounds like a relaxing summer pastime—or maybe a cliché online dating profile, depending on who you ask. But in the case of the annual conference hosted by Novelists, Inc. (NINC), the concept has become a productive, professional five-day event that balances traditional and indie spheres, business and fun. And this year, with the arrival of Hurricane Ian three days after the final meetings wrapped up, it couldn't have taken place at a better time.

Even though I attended this year's NINC Conference for the first time as an industry guest, as a primarily nonfiction writer, I was still able to experience all it offered for attendees. The conference was held on St. Pete Beach, a barrier island on the gulf coast of Florida near St. Petersburg. Although the event officially began September 21 with registration and an opening reception, for those who arrived early, a group of attendees went on a pub crawl the evening prior, and another had a mini conference for their group.

Thursday, Friday, and Saturday were filled from breakfast to NINC After Dark with sessions, meals, and events, many of which were included and sponsored by various industry leaders. Many attendees scheduled meetings with the sponsors during their office hours and overall seemed to plan their time at NINC more than I've observed at other conferences. This surprised me at first, but it makes sense when you consider that these are very serious, business-minded authors. They are where they are in their careers because they have worked hard, and the conference is no exception.

Still, they played equally hard in the evenings! It was surprising yet a perfect balance that was better than any other conference I've been to in any industry. There's a strong effort to provide something on site for everyone throughout the event, as they understand that the networking at more casual events can be just as important to an author's career trajectory as the sessions. You can come and go as you like and tailor your conference experience to your needs.

Sunday morning, September 25, was the business meeting for members only, though many attendees were making plans to leave earlier than they had planned anyway because of the increasing threat of Hurricane Ian. Fortunately, all were able to leave in time, and the resorts appear to have survived well and will be ready for us in 2023.

WHAT IS NINC?

NINC is the premier organization for high-powered novelists. It was formed over thirty years ago and has grown into a global community of over a thousand authors committed to the business of writing. Originally just for traditionally published authors, the organization has since broadened their membership requirements to allow indie authors to join—now, around 85 percent of members are self-published, and 72 percent are traditionally published, according to the website.

With members that each have an average of fifteen years of experience in the industry and twenty-four published books to their name, NINC's membership criteria are designed to maintain the focus on high-level conversations and information that comes with multiple successful novels published. That said, they are a welcoming group of people and hope that if you don't qualify now, you soon will.

They've had an annual conference since nearly the inception of the organization. According to Barbara Keiler, a former president, the event used to move from place to place until they eventually settled on their current location in St. Pete Beach, Florida, each September. The conference typically begins Wednesday evening and goes through the organization's business meeting Sunday morning.

HIGH POINTS

More than most conferences I've attended in various industries, NINC provides multiple opportunities for attendees to have quality conversations with sponsors and industry vendors. For several authors I met, this was key for their continued business success, and many were instrumental in getting features added to our favorite platforms that benefit all of us. Many of the sponsors and industry professionals have industry suite hours. These are similar to office hours, where attendees can get their questions answered by the representatives of the company. The companies also listened to the requests of the attendees—in fact, many new features are rolled out as a result of requests made at these meetings every year. And you can often catch them in the lobby or attending sessions and events as well.

Marketing and business development sessions were prominent, as were multiple craft sessions and roundtable discussions during NINC After Dark, when attendees grabbed a favorite beverage and dessert and sat ten to a table with others who write in a similar genre or had questions about a particular topic. The discussion was free-flowing and unscripted, with two rounds about an hour each Wednesday through Friday nights. Saturday night was a beach blowout with dinner and drinks catered on the beach.

Peer-to-peer conversations often occurred in the lobby and other areas of the venue. I overheard conversations that potentially shifted the entire trajectory of an author's business and heard even more stories of such conversations in years past.

Although I attended as an industry guest, I still came away with some great takeaways to apply to my own authorial journey. In Janet Margot's session on Amazon Ads, I realized what I've done wrong in my Amazon Ads and feel confident that they will perform better for me in the future by applying what she recommended. I was excited, as were many other attendees, to learn that you can now go direct with audio as well as e-books with BookFunnel. I regretted later not going to the Google Play session, but I heard many authors talking about their excitement over the rollout of new AI narration for audio and the potential for utilizing Spotify and Findaway Voices in their businesses.

Session topics ranged from marketing to tools and platforms, craft, business, and mindset and wellness. Multiple sessions occur at the same time, and it is often difficult to choose, but NINC secures official session notetakers who provide the notes on all the sessions to their members. I'd not heard of this service before, but I was impressed with the organization's attention to detail in ensuring the best outcome for every attendee. In fact, many authors told me they don't try to take their own notes at the conference and instead just jot down task-list items inspired by the sessions.

As with any author conference, there is no substitute for being with people in the same place at the same time. NINC, as with most of the rest of the world, went virtual during COVID-19, and many attendees commented on how good it was to be with their fellow writers again. Often, while the official events are excellent, it's the chance conversation held in between sessions that can make all the difference in the world to your career. And NINC 2022 will go down in many author's careers as landmark events that made all the difference.

If you're a novelist of at least two works more than thirty thousand words, be they traditionally and/or indie published, and meet their advance and royalty numbers—an advance of two thousand dollars if traditionally published, or income of five thousand dollars if indie—this is an organization well worth your time and investment, as is the conference. Set five thousand dollars as a royalty goal, apply for membership by May 31, and sign up as quickly as you can—if it's anything like this year's, 2023's conference will be well worth the investment.

Alice Briggs

A Peek Behind the Table

HOW TO PREPARE FOR YOUR FIRST SIGNING EVENT AS AN AUTHOR

There's nothing quite as exhilarating as readers flowing through an event, stopping at your booth or table, asking questions about your books, and exchanging money for an autographed copy. Although ads, marketing, and social media are all useful tools in your marketing belt, book fairs and events are probably the most exciting way to get your name and books into the world. You have a chance for a few hours to put yourself and your creativity on display, create bonds with potential readers, and network with other authors, some of whom will become friends for life. Yet as fun as these events are, they also can be daunting, especially if you're new to the book-signing world and aren't sure how to prepare for one.

Not to fear—we've got everything you need to consider ahead of time, so you can feel confident enough to start practicing your signature.

NOT YOUR PARENTS' BOOK SIGNING

There are many types of events you can attend as an author, and while some of them are obvious, others may be more outside the box. Event Coordinators (ECs) across the world provide locations where authors can sign in the same venue. Some of these events are for specific genres, but some are multi-genre. They can include planned dinners or parties, tours of local spots, panels for authors to speak, or classes for authors and readers. Don't forget that signings have booth or table rental fees, portions of which may not be refundable, so you'll want to check into those before committing to a signing. Also, it's wise to include the gamut of costs into your budget: books to bring, table decor, hotels, travel costs, food, and more. These can add up quickly if you're not prepared.

Facebook groups, such as Author Events Around the World, feature posts from ECs about event opportunities, as well as posts from authors who are selling their tables at an event they aren't able to attend. Some ECs, like Anytime Author Promotions (https://anytimeauthorpromotions.com), are well known for their events throughout the year and are always adding new locations that draw in readers from across the country, such as authors signing in cells in haunted prisons or patient rooms in haunted asylums. Many events hosted by ECs also contain raffles in which proceeds go to a local charity or other events that directly benefit specific charitable groups, like Authors and Dancers Against Cancer and Scares That Care AuthorCon.

Comic cons are also a fantastic place to sign books that authors often overlook. Because of the nature of these conventions, they will almost always have certain genres that sell better than others. Horror typically sells exceptionally well at most cons, but if you're at an event centered on Fantasy or Sci-Fi, it's best to only rent a booth if you write in those genres. Genres such as Romance— or adjacent genres that involve heavy romance on the

side—almost never mix with a comic con, so if that's what you write, you'll want to avoid a con. You can always check out the previous year's merchants to find out if your genre will mesh with the general audience.

LOCAL EVENTS

If you're newer to book signings, larger events with other authors can give you practical experience signing, along with the opportunity to hone your table display and get advice from seasoned authors. Large events, however, are not the only way to sell books in public. For authors dipping their toes into the world of book events for the first time, taking part in something local can seem more manageable and help you connect with readers in your community.

Almost anywhere can make a great locale for signing with others. Some of these signings may not be set up yet; your area may just need their own EC. Farmers' markets, art fairs, library-organized signings, and community events, such as Oktoberfest or a Renaissance fair, can all have opportunities to rent a booth or table. Join groups within your city or town to stay up to date on local events in your area. Check in with the chamber of commerce in your area about any upcoming fairs

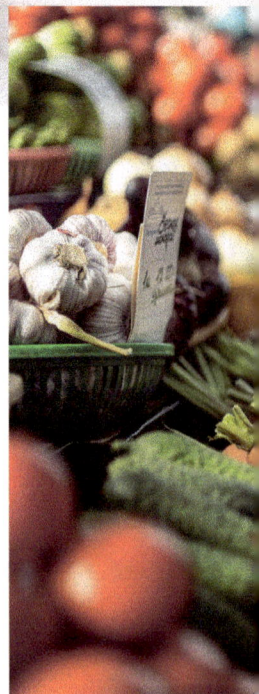

or to get on the list for future events. Newspapers or city magazines may also contain information about upcoming events that may provide an opportunity to sell books. Stop by libraries or bookstores as well to inquire about signing events by local authors.

Even if your library doesn't have an event planned, consider whether you'd be willing to help organize something on your own. This is where experience with other signing events can come in handy. Volunteer to work with the library to create a new event for local authors. Advertise through Facebook groups, newspapers, radio stations, or other outlets. The same idea goes for local art fairs. If your area doesn't already have one, contact the chamber of commerce about creating a new yearly event. Don't limit yourself to what's already established.

GENRE MATTERS

Just like with comic cons, before scheduling a signing with other authors, ensure you've signed up for an event that aligns with the kinds of stories you write. You won't want to attend Naughty in Nashville if you write primarily Thrillers. Some events also require you to write a specific genre to attend. If you have any doubts about how well your genre matches after reading about the event, contact the EC to ensure you're signing up for the right one for your books.

There are some events that sound genre-specific in the title but will allow all genres. However, Horror author Carver Pike, who also writes Romance books under the pen name CM Genovese, says you can use this to your advantage in certain situations. When Pike attends a Horror signing, he will only bring his Horror novels with him because Horror readers do not tend to read Romance; however, for a Romance signing, he always brings his Horror titles as well. "A lot of Romance readers will and do also read Horror," he says. "Also, some Romance readers drag their husbands or significant others along with them and that person might not like Romance at all, but they might like Horror."

PREPARE FOR EVERYTHING

Once you've booked a signing event, preparation is key, not only when deciding what to bring with you but also when communicating with an EC regarding any needs you might have. Even if the venue is halfway across the country, most ECs provide an address where you can mail books, or you can mail them directly to the venue. Most authors recommend bringing approximately ten to fifteen copies of each book, depending on the length of your backlist. If you're an author with fifteen novels, identify your best sellers and bring more of those than others. If you only have two novels, you can easily bring twenty copies of each. The expected attendance size of the event also factors into how many books to bring. If it's a small event, consider bringing fewer, but if it's a large event with projections of three hundred readers, consider bringing extra copies of your more popular titles.

If you have a disability or need specific accommodations, coordinate with your EC in advance regarding arrangements for parking, table location, assistance with unloading or setup, or starting setup early. If you suffer from something like epilepsy, make the EC and venue aware in case you need medical help.

Author Autumn Marie writes that authors should consider everything, including how to get from point A to point B at the event location. As a wheelchair user, she's had to get creative with transporting materials to and from her booths at events—she uses a wagon to tow her materials around and connects it to her wheelchair with a large S hook. "Set up can sometimes be a challenge, but I never back away from a good challenge," she writes. "I try to get there early for set up because my cart is not the only thing on wheels … I am, too. I have no problem asking for help if I need it, because sometimes I do." You will want to have an assistant at the event who understands your disability and can assist. Marie writes most ECs are very understanding and willing to help those with disabilities, even those in wheelchairs, but to ask for assistance from ECs well in advance so they can plan to accommodate you.

A FINAL WORD

Signings can be daunting, whether it's your first or tenth, a group of fifty authors or only five. Just remember to have fun, Pike says, and that you're likely not the only one who's anxious. "You'll be nervous. That's natural. Everyone is a little nervous, especially for their first signing. Readers are nervous too. They'll be the first to tell you." Marie's largest bit of advice is to slow down and make new friends. The more you enjoy the event and get to know others, the easier it will be to do the next signing and maybe even one day host your own. ■

Angie Martin

The Dos and Don'ts of Creating Your Reader Magnet

No doubt you will see plenty of them with Black Friday and the holiday shopping season underway. In recent years, businesses have begun offering deals and offers through promotional emails to connect with customers and get them spending more. And if you have ever signed up for a retailer's emails in order to get a "20% off your first order" coupon or a restaurant's mailing list to get a free soda, you have succumbed to a lead magnet as well.

As an author, you can use this tactic to grow your email list too. The idea is simple: Offer something of value, such as a short story or even a full-length novel, for free in exchange for an email address. This free incentive is known as a reader magnet, and it's a favorite method for many indie authors for growing a mailing list and appealing to new audiences.

In the early days of the internet it was often enough to invite people to sign up for news and updates, but with 300 billion emails now being sent every day, according to Radicati, our inboxes are overflowing, and that incentive doesn't cut it anymore. We are all much more cautious about who we share our email address with, so the appeal of your reader magnet is vitally important. Here are a few dos and don'ts to keep in mind when creating yours.

Lorem ipsum dolor sit amet, consectetur adipisicing elit, sed do eiusmod tempor incididunt ut labore et dolore magna aliqua. Ut enim ad minim veniam, quis nostrud exercitation ullamco laboris nisi ut aliquip ex ea commodo consequat. Duis aute irure dolor in reprehenderit in voluptate velit esse cillum dolore eu fugiat nulla pariatur. Excepteur sint occaecat cupidatat non proident, sunt in culpa qui officia deserunt mollit anim id est laborum. Sed ut perspiciatis unde omnis iste natus error sit voluptatem accusantium doloremque laudantium, totam rem aperiam, eaque ipsa quae ab illo inventore veritatis et quasi architecto beatae vitae dicta sunt explicabo. Nemo enim ipsam voluptatem quia voluptas sit aspernatur aut odit aut fugit, sed quia consequuntur magni dolores eos qui ratione voluptatem sequi nesciunt. Neque porro quisquam est, qui dolorem ipsum quia dolor sit amet, consectetur, adipisci velit, sed quia non numquam eius modi tempora incidunt ut labore et dolore magnam aliquam quaerat

DO GET CREATIVE

There are many reasons you may not want to give away a full book—perhaps you're still writing your first one or you feel strongly that you don't want to give away your creative work for free. Although your reader magnet should ideally give readers a taste of your writing and/or story world, there are other options for reader magnets besides books if you're willing to get creative.

Pro Tip: Bradley Charbonneau shares several ideas for alternative reader magnet formats in the June 2022 issue of *Indie Author Magazine*, and Smart Authors Lab offers a few more at https://smartauthorslab. com/reader-magnet-ideas.

If you're trying to attract brand new readers who are not familiar with your writing, it's best to offer something standalone that doesn't require readers to have any prior knowledge of your books. Keep those alternate endings, deleted chapters, or character backstories to include in the back of your books. Then, use these as separate reader magnets to attract existing fans of your work back to your mailing list.

DON'T GIVE AWAY A SAMPLE CHAPTER

While you don't need to give away a full book, a free chapter is not of great value to readers. If they know upfront they're only getting one chapter, they may be less inclined to sign up because they know they will have to buy the book to read the rest. On the other hand, if they didn't realize it was only a sample chapter, it may irritate them to find that they have to buy the full book at the end.

It's okay to give away a free chapter as a placeholder while you come up with something else, but aim to replace it with something complete as soon as you can. The length of your reader magnet is less important than how well it engages your reader—give away a short novella or even a one-page story if you feel it "sells" your writing well. The value is not in how much you give away but in how well it satisfies your new subscriber and gets them excited about reading more of your work.

DO APPEAL TO THE RIGHT READERS

You will also want to check that your reader magnet is going to attract the right readers. You may have a high quality short story that you're happy to give away, but if it's in a different genre to the books you have for sale, it may not be the best fit.

Many authors offer a prequel to a series as a reader magnet. This can work well to give subscribers a taste of what is to come and get them interested in the characters. This type of reader magnet is especially effective when at least the first book in the series is already available and your new subscribers can buy it as soon as they have finished the prequel.

DON'T GIVE AWAY SUB-PAR WORK

Keep in mind that if new subscribers don't enjoy your reader magnet, they are unlikely to a) engage with your emails or b) buy your books. Make sure your reader magnet is of high quality and a good representation of your writing. Treat your freebie as you would any other work you publish—invest in editing and/or proofreading, and invite feedback from beta readers before you share it with your audience.

DO MAKE A GOOD FIRST IMPRESSION

In short, try to make life easy for yourself. Your reader magnet is important, but it is also free, so don't feel pressured to write a full-length novel just to give it away. Repurpose stories you already have, or offer something that isn't a story at all if that's easier. Consider recipes, audio playlists, or maps, for example. Just be wary of cutting corners and think about what's in it for your readers. Your reader magnet is often your first impression, and first impressions count. ■

Belinda Griffin

#Unfiltered

WHAT AUTHORS SAY ONLINE MATTERS TO THEIR READERS, SO HOW MUCH SHOULD YOU BE SHARING ON SOCIAL MEDIA?

Being a writer never stops. If you're not writing, you're often thinking about it. If you're not doing either, you're likely to be looking at cover designs, formatting, talking to other authors—the list goes on.

And that's before you even get to marketing your work, whether through blogging, promo stacking, newsletter swaps, or social media. But that last one can feel like a separate beast all on its own. Social media platforms provide a unique chance for authors to interact with their readers on a more personal level, but they can make it even more difficult to balance what your audience sees of your life beyond your writing career.

Obviously, if social media is something you include in your marketing, you have to find the time for it, but it's even more important to decide which platforms you should use and what you want to share with your audience—or what they want to see from you.

The answers to these can vary, but they're crucial to consider when shaping and maintaining your author brand. And although we can't give you a right way to manage your social media presence, we can help you understand what other authors are doing and why it matters so you can decide which options are right for you.

PICK YOUR PLATFORMS

Social media is ever changing, with new platforms, algorithms, and trends constantly coming and going. It can be difficult to choose which platforms are best for growing and connecting with your audience. A report by DataReportal (https://datareportal.com/social-media-users) in August of this year lists eighteen top social sites, though there are many smaller ones as well. That said, certain platforms currently vie for some of

the top spots when ranked by number of active users, depending on your region and the demographics you're trying to reach.

Facebook is the largest social media platform in the world with almost 3 billion users, according to DataReportal. Instagram is also up there with almost 1.5 billion users. Both platforms are owned by the same parent company, Meta; however, Instagram also has the benefit of an established, active reading community. To date, users have shared more than 81 million posts using the #Bookstagram hashtag to connect with other readers, making it easy for authors to reach their target audiences by doing the same.

TikTok reached a billion users in 2021 and is still growing. According to TikTok's own statistics, seventy percent of users agree that "they feel a deeper connection to people they interact with on TikTok than on other platforms," and two out of three users are likely to buy something while using the platform. In fact, selling books on TikTok has become so significant that Nielsen, Forbes, and Bloomberg have all covered the platform's impact on the book industry this year.

Twitter has only 486 million users, in comparison, but it is growing and has 31.8 million monetizable daily active users, which has grown 15.4 percent since its 2021 second-quarter report. Like Instagram, Twitter also hosts an active reading community, which has grown in recent years through the use of hashtags like #booktwitter, #booktwt, and #writerwednesday.

Of course, not every platform works well in connecting to readers in every genre. As you consider where to build your social media presence, look at where you're most likely to find readers based on each site's demographics and where other authors in your genre have built their audiences. Then think about the kinds of content you prefer to make and what you're likely to keep up with. If you hate creating videos, there's no point in focusing on TikTok or any other video-based platform.

The key to good social media performance is consistency. You need to show up and post regularly to keep yourself and your books at the top of people's minds, so to start, choose fewer platforms to focus on rather than trying to spread yourself thin over every platform.

DECIDE WHAT YOU WANT TO SHARE

Once you've decided where to reach your readers, you'll also need to consider what to share with them. Some authors let it all hang out on social media. They share health issues, family goings-on, and their thoughts and opinions on everything under the sun. Others stick to sharing only book news, teasers on what's coming next, writing inspiration, and other author-related news. Still others find a balance somewhere in the middle.

Which one is right? There is no right or wrong, only what you are comfortable with. Don't feel you have to share everything if you don't want to. Equally, don't feel you have to keep quiet if you want to share. However, here's what you need to think about when making your decision:

What do your readers enjoy?

Do they like hearing your latest shenanigans?

Do they want to get to know you better or would they rather you just post book news?

When you post on social media, you are developing your author brand. If you share too much outside of what readers have come to expect of you, will that affect your brand negatively? It's worth considering, whether you're just starting out or you've been posting on social media for years.

As you're finding the answers to the questions above, try posts with different content to see which get the most interaction, or simply ask your followers what they prefer to see. The results will help give you a better idea of what your audience likes and what you should prioritize sharing with your readers.

SPEAK YOUR MIND (OR DON'T)

For those who choose a more open-door approach to what they share online, it's best to consider ahead of time whether you'll make public any of your more personal beliefs. According to the 2020 Consumer Culture Report by 5WPR, an independent public relations agency, 83 percent of millennials want

companies to "align with their values." Seventy-six percent would also like CEOs to talk about issues they are passionate about, and 62 percent would rather have products from companies that show what they stand for politically and socially.

That's pretty clear. However, it is also the case, from the same report, that 65 percent of millennials have boycotted a company that didn't share their views on particular issues. Although the percentages are lower for older generations, it's still the case that over half of people at any age prefer to support companies that share their values.

Everyone has strong opinions on certain things. We've all seen battles break out and sides drawn on the internet over everything from whether Star Wars or Star Trek is better to far more serious and controversial topics, such as the striking down of Roe v. Wade.

Whichever way you lean on the big issues, you will invariably lose readers if you make your opinions known. Someone somewhere will disagree with what you have to say, but those readers you gain are more likely to stick around and appreciate you. The only other consideration is how much you feel you can keep quiet on any controversial issues that arise—particularly when staying quiet could be seen as support for views and ideas you would never tolerate.

It's not a simple decision to make, but only you know how comfortable you feel talking about big issues, whether those conversations fit in with your author brand, and whether you're okay with losing readers who don't agree with you.

BE CONSISTENT

No matter where you build your platform or what you decide to share with your readers, understand that your decisions will create expectations among your audience and become part of your author brand. You might be known for gloriously funny Rom-Coms and a sharp wit on your social platforms too. You might be the go-to writer for deeply dark and disturbing Horror tales, with gallows humor to match in person.

What you need to be on your website and social

platforms is consistent. Wherever you post, use the same username, if possible, on every platform to make yourself easier to find. Try to keep the same look and feel to your posts. Readers should be able to look at your posts and immediately recognize that it's you before they've read what you've said. That's strong branding, and it helps with your marketing by building brand recognition.

Finally, try to post consistently. If there have been tumbleweed blowing across your social accounts for months, don't be surprised if no one's interested when you have a book out.

Research your chosen platforms' algorithms and find out what the recommended number of posts is per week, then try to post at least the minimum number on each platform.

KEEP IT UP

Creating an initial social media plan can offer plenty of challenges already, but when deadlines creep closer or other life responsibilities get in the way, it can be hard to stick to the consistent posting schedule you create. Still, with a little planning and some additional software, you can make it work.

Some authors choose to plan out their social posts for each quarter rather than creating posts individually. If you don't have time to do that, at least try to plan out the upcoming month, as creating posts in batches can save time and help ensure your content is cohesive across your accounts. If the software is within your budget, social-media-scheduling programs, such as MeetEdgar, HootSuite, and CoSchedule, allow users to create a calendar of prepared posts and queue evergreen content to repost regularly.

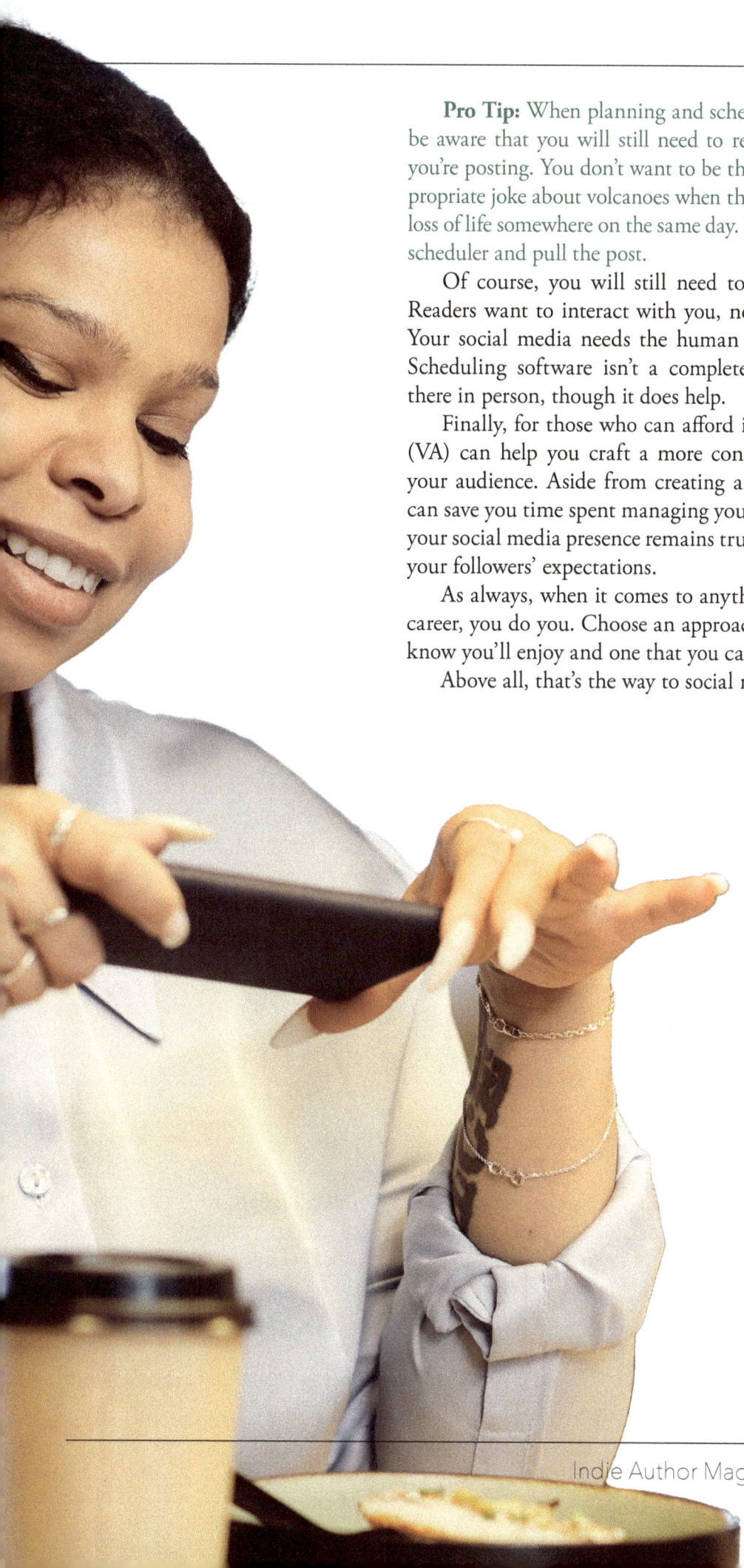

Pro Tip: When planning and scheduling posts ahead of time, be aware that you will still need to regularly keep track of what you're posting. You don't want to be the writer who posts an inappropriate joke about volcanoes when there's a serious eruption with loss of life somewhere on the same day. If you need to, log into your scheduler and pull the post.

Of course, you will still need to interact live occasionally. Readers want to interact with you, not just with your software. Your social media needs the human element to make it work. Scheduling software isn't a complete substitute for you being there in person, though it does help.

Finally, for those who can afford it, hiring a virtual assistant (VA) can help you craft a more consistent online presence for your audience. Aside from creating and scheduling posts, a VA can save you time spent managing your accounts and help ensure your social media presence remains true to your author brand and your followers' expectations.

As always, when it comes to anything related to your author career, you do you. Choose an approach to social media that you know you'll enjoy and one that you can maintain long term.

Above all, that's the way to social media success that lasts. ■

Gill Fernley

Four Free, Easy-to-Use Programs for Every Stage of Publishing

If you're like many indies, you didn't jump into writing and publishing full time with a limitless budget for your startup expenses. Plenty of us need to make careful financial choices and spend based on items classified as needs rather than wants.

But that doesn't mean that there aren't excellent free options for the bootstrapping author-turned-entrepreneur. To help ease the burden, here are four tools that don't require any initial investment yet can help in every stage of an author's business.

EVERNOTE

Evernote has evolved from a simple notetaking application to an all-in-one organization system that can connect your email, calendar, notes, links, meetings, and file storage in one central dashboard. Two features in particular make it a standout: It's easily added as a stand-alone app to any mobile or desktop device, and it has a broad set of integration capabilities with common apps like Gmail, Outlook, Google Drive, and Slack.

Evernote can be especially helpful for creating character or location sketches with multimedia. As you surf the web researching information about your next project, Evernote's Web Clipper can be used to create bookmarks for articles and websites to reference later. You can also save the entire article, images included, into a single note. You can drag and drop images into a note; add audio files, videos, or whole PDFs for a complete profile; and use templates to standardize what's included in each note.

As items are added to Evernote, they become searchable. Writers can also group multiple notes into stacks to create a story bible that contains their research, character sketches, documents, and tasks in one place.

Evernote's free version comes with a basic feature set, including the Web Clipper, but it has upload and file size limitations and restricts synchronization to two devices. Upgrading to the Personal Plan for $7.99 per month allows for increased file sizes, calendar integration, and reminders and tasks, as well as the ability to sync unlimited devices.

Pro Tip: Connect your dictation app to Evernote to keep backups of your raw text files, which you can then copy to your writing app for editing.

DESCRIPT

One technique for increased word counts is to dictate your first draft, transcribe the audio file to text, and then polish it during the editing process. Apple and Android devices already have options for creating voice files and saving them as MP3 files. Once the audio files are recorded, many programs offer a basic built-in transcription feature, including the online version of Microsoft Word. However, the accuracy and collaboration features of Descript consistently rank higher than other commercial competitors, without the need to train the app as is required in other programs, such as in Dragon Naturally Speaking.

Beyond its accuracy as a transcription tool, some of Descript's most useful features are the editing tools you can employ before copying the transcript into your word-processing app. Descript adds paragraph breaks and punctuation without the need to dictate them into your audio file, and the software also comes with a feature to remove filler words like "um," "ah," and "so." The app can even identify and replace instances of a personal filler word, such as "like."

Nonfiction writers or podcasters that conduct interviews have even more shiny objects to play with. Descript can automatically identify different speakers and create captions, and it offers an overdub feature that creates an AI version of your own voice. You provide the transcript, and the program will generate an AI audio file.

The free version of the program comes with three hours of transcription and a trial of the advanced features. The full version of Descript costs 30 dollars per month and includes ten hours of transcription. However, the program also provides users the option to upgrade in only the months they might need more, then downgrade back to the free version when three hours is enough.

Pro Tip: Streamline your dictation workflow using Zapier. When you add an audio file to a Dropbox folder or Google Drive folder, you can automatically request it be transcribed and ready for you to edit in minutes.

REEDSY BOOK EDITOR

Every writer has their own preferred writing tool, whether it be Scrivener, Microsoft Word, Google Docs, or the old-school pen and paper. Each has an extensive feature list for writers to play with. However, if you're on a budget and looking for a well-rounded app that gives you writing, collaborative editing, and formatting in one tool, Reedsy might be a good choice.

As free apps go, the Reedsy Book Editor is no slouch on features. It's accessible via a web browser, which means it's the same interface whether you use a PC, Mac, or mobile device. You can import a Microsoft Word document or create a new document from scratch and create chapters, parts, and scenes.

Some of Scrivener's popular features, such as goals, daily word trackers, and insights, are easy to set. Like Google Docs and Microsoft Word, Reedsy includes a "track changes" feature and a way to send a link to collaborators to read and comment, which can be handy when alpha readers or editors need to chime in.

When you're ready to export, the interface also gives you simple choices for EPUB and print files. The program already includes styles that readers expect to see, such as drop caps and paragraph indentations, and doesn't require you to fiddle with settings to get them to work correctly. Use the built-in templates for simple styles, or you can choose to download a formatted DOCX file if you prefer to use a different formatting tool, like Vellum.

Even better? Reedsy Book Editor is entirely free to use with a full feature set and no need for paid upgrades.

Pro Tip: For a more complete overview, watch the replay of Reedsy's Author Tech Summit session from September 2022: https://authortech-summit.com/lessons/webinar-reedsy-book-editor/

BEEFREE.IO

Email service providers (ESPs) such as MailerLite, Mailchimp, SendFox, and Sendinblue all have similar drag-and-drop interfaces for designing emails. These can be helpful, as can the templates that most include for holidays or special circumstances, but many of them can feel like generic design options. Moreover, when you're trying to stand out from a crowd, sending an email using the same template as fifteen other authors in the same week—"Gobble Gobble This Book Deal!"—isn't ideal.

BeeFree Pro boasts over 1,240 email templates that can be customized and used with any ESP. Some ESPs have direct integrations, pushing the finished design over as a draft you can open, edit, and send to your saved audiences. If your ESP doesn't offer direct integration, you can export the entire email as a ZIP file with the images included, or you can copy and paste the final HTML and leave the images hosted on BeeFree's servers.

Beyond the design features, the emails that are produced are desktop and mobile friendly. There are options for inserting your own ESP's merge fields for personalization, and you can send test emails to collaborators for comments and feedback. The comments are then available to view alongside the test email in the app.

The free version of the program comes with ten emails, unlimited exports, and unlimited collaborators. Emails can be individual emails, or you can create your own template to use multiple times. Users can upgrade to the Pro version for 30 dollars per month to access unlimited emails and the ability to save blocks of content for reuse, like social media icons or footer information. Those with paid upgrades can also remove the "created with Bee" tag from the bottom of their emails and will have access to email support.

Pro Tip: Create your primary newsletter template and edit it in BeeFree each time you send your newsletter. Editing a single email doesn't count toward your free limit.

As the CEO of your career, making good financial decisions is a must. Filling your author toolbox with the right set of free tools can help you streamline your operations without sacrificing quality, increasing your workload, or breaking the bank. ■

Chelle Honiker

Do you have a tool you'd like to share? Tell us about it on our website at: https://indieauthormagazine.com/ feedback

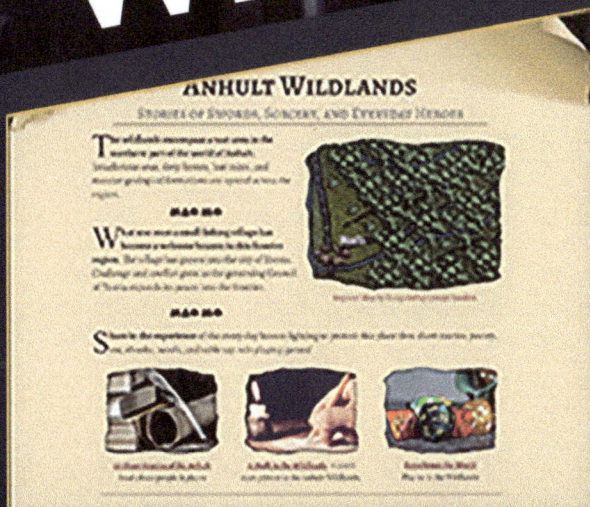

Tech Tools

Courtesy of IndieAuthorTools.com
Got a tool you love and want to share with us?
Submit a tool at IndieAuthorTools.com

SIGNATURE HOUND

https://signaturehound.com/
Email signatures made easy! Create an account and build a custom email signature using your brand colors, fonts, social media links and more. Comes with templates for polished looks, and instructions for use in most of the email apps like Gmail, Outlook, and Office 365.

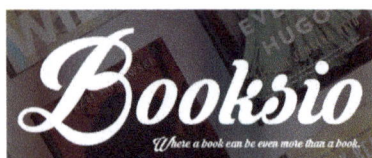

BOOKSIO

https://booksio.sjv.io/x9M1Wx
We know you probably have at least a dozen places to buy books and magazines from. Why do you need Booksio? The obvious answer is our giving – ten percent of every Booksio purchase goes to a charitable organization. We have over 16 million titles available, covering print books, digital books and magazines, and audiobooks, so you will find your next favorite story.

BOOKSWEEPS

https://www.booksweeps.com/authors/
BookSweeps provides marketing tools and turnkey promotions to help you grow an audience for your writing. A catalog of great features makes BookSweeps the most popular lead generation and discoverability platform for authors and publishers of all stripes.

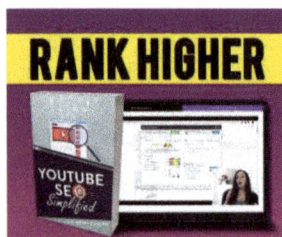

THE YOUTUBE SEO SIMPLIFIED SYSTEM

https://appsumo.8odi.net/QO30qY
Learn how to earn more money from your author YouTube channel by ranking your videos higher in search results. The YouTube SEO Simplified System is a complete step-by-step online video training program. Bonus materials, including free 90-day access to TubeBuddy, are included.

REEDSY BOOK EDITOR

https://authortechsummit.com/lessons/webinar-reedsy-book-editor/
With Reedsy Book Editor you can write, edit, and typeset your manuscript, and export it to PDF and ePUB easily. And with collaboration features to rival Google Docs soon, it could become your new indispensable tool.

Making the List

HOW YOUR BOOK COULD BE THE NEXT BESTSELLER

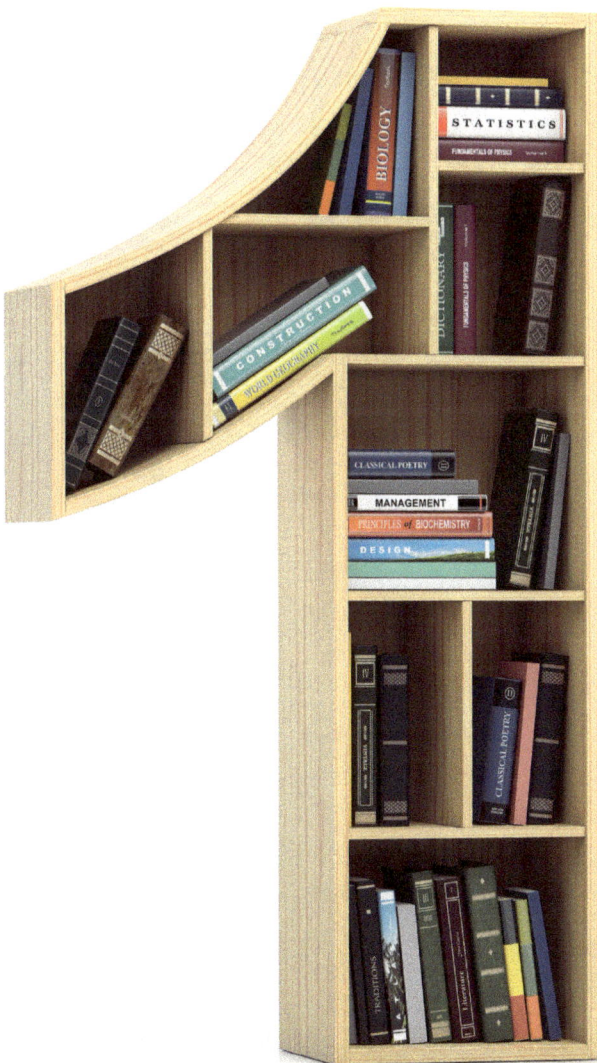

Some see attaining bestseller status as a pinnacle of author success. Whether for the publicity it can provide for their work or the sense of achievement it can bring on a more personal level, nearly every author dreams of one day having their title immortalized on one of the most prestigious lists known to publishing. But how can you achieve this monument, and what are the risks involved? In this article, we'll examine what a bestseller list is, as well as some of the requirements you'll need to know in order to partake in a bestseller run of your own.

WHAT THE BESTSELLER LIST ISN'T

Bestseller lists aren't the most accurate depictions of sales numbers. Some lists, such as The New York Times Bestseller List, are curated, which means organizers choose titles based on a variety of factors about the book and not just how many copies it sells. The methodology for choosing books that will be on the bestseller list varies by the organizations that publish them. In fact, some titles that are listed as bestsellers for multiple weeks only sell hundreds of copies, not thousands, according to multiple authors in a 2018 report by EPJ Data Science. Additionally, not all bestseller lists will include self-published titles in their initial data pools.

Keep in mind that making the top of Amazon lists and categories does not equal bestseller status either. Amazon often discourages authors from calling themselves "Amazon Bestsellers," to where it will potentially remove books from sale that include the term on their cover copy or on their sales page.

So if the lists are so heavily skewed, why attempt to have your book listed? Although some lists have been curated by organizers, other bestseller lists are strictly based on numbers and therefore provide equal opportunities for all authors. These are the lists that are most viable for indie authors. If you're interested in attaining a bestseller title, it is best to focus on lists that are created by publications such as USA TODAY and Wall Street Journal, who often list indie writers among their rankings.

WHY BESTSELLER LISTS MATTER

A variety of authors choose to focus on sales instead of attaining a spot on a bestseller list, which is a valid goal. After all, an author can sell thousands of copies of their books without attaining bestseller status and still make a good income. What makes a bestseller title important is the benefits it can have for your career overall.

If used properly, a bestseller title can

- bolster your acceptance rate for advertising promotions, such as BookBub deals;
- enhance your chances at gaining featured slots with Kobo, Barnes & Noble, and other distributors;
- increase your viability for signing a print-exclusive deal with traditional publishers;
- help you be accepted as a signing author at exclusive book conventions and land speaking engagements;
- make your name more recognizable for awards and competitions;
- open pathways for potential contracts that lead outside of publishing, such as film rights; and
- give credibility to your work.

Attaining bestseller status opens doors for indie authors that were previously closed to them. Striving to achieve a "bestseller" ranking for your work isn't so much a money-making strategy as it is a long-term investment in your career, providing avenues to both make an income and gain opportunities from nontraditional methods once you have the achievement in hand.

BESTSELLER REQUIREMENTS

There are a variety of bestseller lists available, and each of them have different requirements your work must meet in order to be listed. Generally, however, it's best to make sure your book meets the following criteria:

- The book is wide and listed on several retailers. It cannot be exclusive to Kindle Unlimited.
- You must gain a minimum of four thousand sales on Amazon and at least three hundred sales on other platforms, whether they be on Apple, Barnes & Noble, Kobo, or elsewhere, though these numbers fluctuate depending on the books released that week. If you go for a list run during a popular time of year for book sales, such as December, you will need to sell more books in order to compete against Christmas sales of other titles.
- These sales numbers must be accumulated in a one-week period, from Monday to Sunday.

E-books, paperbacks, and hardcovers all count toward a book's sales data. In most situations, audiobooks do not count toward sales numbers for bestseller lists, though this may change in the future.

HOW TO HAVE A BESTSELLER RUN

Receiving a ranking on a bestseller list is no small feat, and in most cases, the achievement takes an incredible amount of hard work, as well as a significant financial investment. The average cost to take on a list run can vary from as little as three thousand dollars to as much as twenty thousand dollars, with no guarantee that it will result in a ranking. Authors have hit—and missed—the lists with such investments, so authors who attempt a list run should first have an established career that can afford the investment.

Many authors attempt to undergo a list run when they've been accepted for a BookBub Featured Deal, in order to enhance their chances of gaining better sales numbers. At other times, it's best to attempt a list-making run during a new release, when your book is most likely to be most exciting to your fan base, or during a sale, so new-to-you readers can give your book a shot without the risk of paying regular price. Booking other promotions, such as newsletter slots, can enhance your chances of making the lists. Asking retailers to feature you, such as applying for Kobo Writing Life Promotions during the week of your run, can give your book enhanced placement on retailers.

Alternatively, several indie authors have attained bestseller status without attempting to be included, such as bestselling Romance author Renee Rose. These authors often hit the lists because of a new release or a big sale that they've announced to their fans. If your reader base is large and they purchase a title of yours all at once, your chances of hitting the list without a designated run increase.

Although list-making can be more complicated than it may seem, attaining status on a bestseller list can be beneficial for an author's career if they understand the benefits it may offer, plan for it carefully, and are willing to take the risk.

This is the first in a series of articles exploring techniques for reaching bestseller status as a self-published author.

Megan Linski-Fox

Podcasts We Love

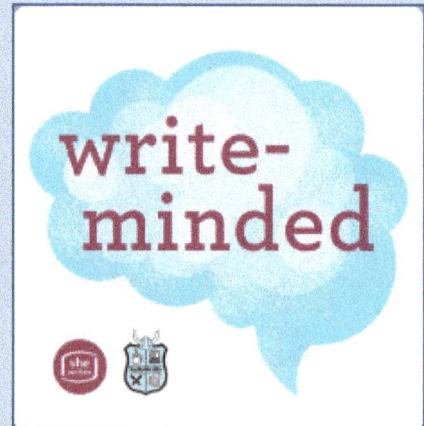

Write-minded: Weekly Inspiration for Writers is a weekly podcast for writers craving a unique blend of inspiration and real talk about the ups and downs of the writing life. Hosted by Brooke Warner of She Writes and Grant Faulkner of National Novel Writing Month (NaNoWriMo), each theme-focused episode of Write-minded features an interview with a writer, author, or publishing industry professional. This year we're featuring a Book Trend at the end of each episode to keep listeners in the loop about what they need to know about the book industry. Brooke and Grant bring to this weekly podcast their shared spirit of community, collaboration, and a deeply held belief that everyone is a writer, and everyone's story matters.
https://podcast.shewrites.com/how-to-listen/

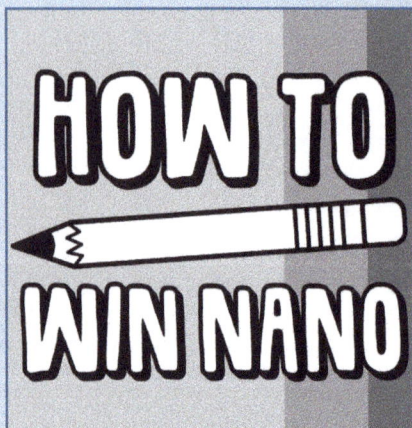

How To Win NaNo is a no-nonsense guide to writing a novel in 30 days. November ticks closer every day, but don't worry — your hosts are here for you! Kristina Horner and Liz Leo are NaNoWriMo experts (and lifelong writing friends) with a passion for helping people tackle National Novel Writing Month. Join them each week as they share their personal tips, tricks and other things they've learned over a decade of consecutive NaNoWriMo wins.
https://www.stitcher.com/show/how-to-win-nano

Prickly Pens Podcast is a platform of discussions with three friends who are also authors on the writing journey: Michelle Monkou, Julia Canchola, Gabby Samuels. During each episode, each co-host will add to the discussion around, not only the writing journey, but issues and topics of our lives.
https://pricklypenspodcast.buzzsprout.com/

More than Words

BUILDING CONVINCING BILINGUAL CHARACTERS

So you want to include a character in your story that's part of a culture you're unfamiliar with or who knows a language you cannot speak. From a diversity standpoint, it's an important endeavor. But what can you do as a writer to ensure that it's a realistic portrayal that enriches the narrative instead of pulling the reader out of it?

The answer starts before you even write a word of dialogue.

KNOW YOUR 'WHY.'

No one speaks any language in a vacuum. Even Americans, who are historically monolingual, don't speak a standard form of English. Instead, America is a collection of dialects shaped by the history, habits, and culture of its people, as well as their outlook on the world.

Individually, we change how and when we speak depending on our social situations. We talk to our friends differently than we would a stranger or colleague. We also tend to adopt the speaking patterns and vocabulary of the people we are most closely associated with, even creating a language based on shared experiences and inside jokes.

In other words, every character you create brings not only their words but also their entire world, culture, and worldview with them when they speak.

When writers ignore this, typically characters lack depth or come off as a stereotype, existing only to show the reader how foreign they are compared with the main character.

SO HOW DO YOU AVOID THIS?

Any character's dialogue reflects not only themselves but their larger environment. When working through your dialogue, consider the following:

- What are the major goals and issues affecting this community?
- What are common knowledge, slang, phrases, or inside jokes that could come up? How does this community communicate with one another when it's just them? What about when they are communicating with people outside the community?
- How do they govern themselves? Is the community matriarchal? Is there a body of elders? How do these rules affect how they engage with people who don't understand their culture?

When writing about a culture or community you're unfamiliar with, research is essential, even regarding dialogue. In worlds built around modern-day settings, podcasts or YouTube videos in which members of the community interact with one another can be a perfect place to start. In other cases, try to find conversations or interactions from those communities recorded in other ways, such as through written records.

No community is a monolith—there are always subgroups within cultures. Consider the differences in language, mannerism, and engagement that could occur when your character interacts with others, even when they speak the same language or come from similar communities. For instance, the Spanish word "pinche," or stingy, translates slightly differently in Mexico than it does in South America, and it means something totally different—and can be considered more vulgar and offensive—in some parts of Spain.

Also consider divisions within a community, such as by class or by age. Class systems exist everywhere, even within the US, and some cultures have strict expectations for how people within different classes, societal roles, or age brackets refer to one another.

WHAT SHOULD IT LOOK LIKE?

Writing multilingual characters takes some research, but it doesn't mean you need to learn a new language altogether. Even common words like "please," "thank you," and "excuse me," as well as declarations of awe, shock, or surprise, can be enough to create realistic and believable dialogue. Just be careful—language ages, so make sure the words you use are from the correct time period.

The screech was replaced with chatter and rolling dice.

"Trois six! Girl, put that with the three ova kind!"

"Nah, man … I already got three of a kind, so I ain't puttin' it there." We could hear her suck her teeth from the other room. "I'm goin' for the big one."

Dice rattled then made muted sounds as they fell on the felt. Screams filled the entire house. Everyone in the living room jumped, their eyes fixed on the teenagers in the other room.

"The les ado are actin' like Ricains over there." My uncle turned to me.

"Rena, tell them to quiet down."

Any other time I woulda run over there and done as I was asked. "I'm American too, tonton."

Additionally, show your character code switching. The term refers to how someone speaks and engages with people of their own culture, family, or close associates in comparison with others, and it can work just as well for your bilingual characters when they have to engage with your story world's common culture.

"Et eux?" JD lifted his chin at the three clear, glossy mounds resting on the grass.

"What about 'em? They literally just sitting there. Laissez les être."

"The mission's to end all of them, not just the ones that attacked us." JD lifted his rifle.

"JD. Rena. What's going on up there?" I could hear Lindsey's smile through my earpiece.

"We have secondary targets on the field. Just clearing them up." JD pulled the trigger.

Bilingual characters view your fictional world through their experiences, from the inside out. So it's key to have a clear vision of what someone from this particular culture adds to your story. Once you know that, knowing the words to use, the emotions you want to elicit, and the story you want to tell through their words will be easier to find. ■

Chrishaun Keller-Hanna

What It Takes to Make

This issue falls as autumn begins, at least in the Northern Hemisphere. But writers invariably set Christmas-themed books amid images of pine trees laden with snowy boughs, despite 50 percent of the world experiencing the height of summer on December 25. It is a statement to the cultural prevalence of this part of the globe over its southern neighbors: Our seasonal tropes dominate certain genres.

Of course, they aren't the only tropes that signify a holiday story. Some genres already cry out for holiday associations. Cozy Mysteries work well with the social events that fill our diaries throughout the year and allow the writer to get creative with the obligatory puns in their books' titles. Look at the charts across the year, and you will notice stories and book covers changing to match the season. Paranormal Mystery books can make a killing during October and November if linked to Halloween or the Day of the Dead. The same goes for Romance, particularly the sweeter variety. Producers pack the Hallmark Channel to bursting with Christmas movies from mid-November onward; meanwhile, first-love stories and coming-of-age shows hold their own just as well in the summer.

It works for other genres too. Many people argue about whether *Die Hard* is a Christmas movie, but no matter which side of the debate you take, the film's popularity is undeniable.

Your Next Book a Holiday Hit

Even three decades after its release, the movie—which was originally based on Roderick Thorp's novel *Nothing Lasts Forever*—tops the charts as the most-watched holiday movie in four states, according to a 2018 study by StreamingObserver. We do not traditionally link Action Thrillers to the holidays, but adding the poignancy of a potentially ruined Christmas adds to the urgency of the story—and makes for some great cinematography. And for atmosphere, you would need to go a long way to beat James Ellroy's 1990 novel *L.A. Confidential* and the 1997 movie of the same name. Christmas features as a key twist in the story, as it fictionalizes the true events of Black Christmas 1951 for narrative effect.

So could your story benefit from linking it to one of the many holidays celebrated in either hemisphere?

Dickens' *A Christmas Carol* is a tale of penance and reconciliation. As a ghost story, it could have been told at any time of the year, but placing it in a specific time and space—a time and space we all recognize and have emotional attachments to—makes the story more powerful. It also means it's revised, reread, and reinterpreted every Christmas, bringing its message to new generations year after year.

Imagine a post-apocalyptic tale set against a yuletide backdrop with sad, battery-powered twinkly fairy lights following a nuclear explosion. It is easy to imagine the threat of a serial killer who only strikes every Fourth of July or a Domestic Thriller that turns as cold as the turkey left-overs after a fraught Thanksgiving meal. The possibilities are endless.

Books can also pull inspiration from holiday traditions, the weather, or just the nature of the holiday season itself. Holidays bring people together, so

consider stories in which feuding families are forced to bury the hatchet, possibly in each other's backs; or in which singles struggle to bring plus ones to a string of summer weddings until they finally find true love themselves.

Think you can't link your books to our world's holidays? Your story world likely has its own festivals and traditions. Shapeshifters, time travelers, space warriors—they can all benefit from rooting their activities around local events and festivities. The Hunger Games are held every year and for some are a time of celebration, feasting, and merriment. Perhaps your dystopian world's arranged marriages have inspired a strange twist on Valentine's Day, or the Chosen One's birthday is marked with celebrations and traditions.

THE HOLIDAY BONUS

For some genres, ensuring you release your books to coincide with a specific holiday could add extra dollars to your bank account. Depending on how quickly you write, you may have to draft your Christmas novel on the United States' Independence Day, July 4, or France's Bastille Day, July 14, when you're surrounded by talk of ice cream sundaes and skinny-dipping in the lake. Just make sure you capitalize on the holiday setting in your cover art and lock down your designs as soon as possible to begin promotion at the end of September.

And even for other genres where the link to the holidays is less commercially obvious, remember that such connections can provide a useful hook on which to hang your hero's journey. We all have an emotional memory of such occasions. All readers will have experienced such events in their own lives, whether good or bad. You may not call your world's tradition "Halloween," but the concept of a time when the veil between worlds is at its thinnest opens up a myriad of storytelling possibilities. Perhaps, in your universe, October 31 marks the beginning of a month of renewal and reflection, where the living stay in their houses and fast while the undead roam the shopping malls and party hard.

Take some time to consider how using the magic, mystery, and sometimes misery of the holidays can work for you as a writer. It might surprise you just how many holiday tales there are still to tell. ■

Susan Odev

No More Winter Woes

WAYS WRITERS CAN COPE WITH SEASONAL AFFECTIVE DISORDER

Many writers are familiar with the winter blues. The cold weather, long periods spent inside, and lack of sunlight can cause feelings of sadness. For some, this can even result in seasonal affective disorder (SAD), a type of seasonal depression that's categorized by a persistently low mood, lack of motivation, and listlessness during certain times of the year, most commonly during the fall and winter months, according to the Mayo Clinic.

But those affected by SAD can combat the disorder with a variety of treatments. One such treatment involves light therapy, or the regular use of a light box that mimics natural light. The light box should be used within the first hour of waking in the morning for about twenty to thirty minutes for maximum effect. Light boxes can be purchased online without a prescription.

Make sure to regulate your sleep and get a good night's rest, as some experts with the National Institute of Mental Health suggest disrupted sleep patterns may contribute to the disorder. Along with getting enough sleep, exercising can help release endorphins that will lift a low mood. Be sure to include plenty of vegetables and fruits in your diet as well.

Writers in particular need to stick to a schedule. Having a daily routine and scheduling regular social outings can provide the same benefits as an active summer calendar. However, don't expect to be at the top of your game if you're impacted by SAD. The year moves in a cycle, and so should authors, with nature thriving in the spring and summer months and easing off to take a break in the fall and winter. If the earth doesn't function at top productivity at all times of the year, authors shouldn't expect to either. Reducing daily word count and using the cold weather months to plan, whether it be plotting new books or arranging signing opportunities, can provide something for authors to look forward to. Much of the discomfort of SAD can be relieved by being more understanding of what your body needs during this time, which is rest and respect for your body's limits.

Finally, if all other methods fail, prescription medications can ease the burden of SAD. If you've tried the above and seen little to no improvement, there are certain medications that can provide a sense of relief. Above all else, talk to your doctor, and be patient in realizing a lack of productivity doesn't mean lost time. Winter teaches us to take it slow and to enjoy the calmer moments in life. Acceptance, along with patience, can bring brighter days again. ■

Megan Linski-Fox

The Imitation Game

IT'S ALL BEEN DONE BEFORE. BUT ONLY YOU CAN DO IT YOUR WAY.

What makes a story original? The question seems simple enough until you try to answer it. Plot alone certainly can't make a book feel unique. Most writing resources agree that the world's stories can be distilled into one of a distinct set of archetypes, though the exact number varies from as low as three, according to author William Foster Harris, to as high as thirty-six, as Georges Polti wrote. Genre categories won't help you stand apart from the crowd much either. The tropes and themes readers expect mean that your story will inevitably be comparable to a neighboring book on the shelf—either that, or it's likely been sorted onto the wrong shelf.

In the art world, a movement known as "postmodernism" suggests that, in fact, creating something entirely original is impossible. The concept was born around 1970 as a reaction to modernism's utopian visions of the future and belief in progress, according to the UK's Tate art gallery. In its stead, postmodernist art no longer embraced defined characteristics and expectations; instead, it broke down barriers and borrowed from the past. Art could be anything, and its originality stemmed as much from the individual experiences of the artist and the viewer as it did from the piece itself.

Authors can view their work in the same light. "With human history dating back hundreds of thousands of years, it is safe to assume that someone, somewhere, at some point in time has done all of this already," wrote Melanie H. Axman in a 2012 article for Business Insider. Plenty of famous stories have come from older versions of the same tale. The modern-day Cinderella came from the Greek story of Rhodopis in the sixth century BCE. Madeline Miller's *The Song of Achilles* came from Homer's *The Iliad*. *The Lion King* came from Shakespeare's *Hamlet*, which came from the Norse legend of Amleth.

Every book will encounter similar themes, characters, or plot points to another that already exists. Stories will be retold under new names and by new authors. Every book will come from the same twenty-six letters, shuffled and reprinted in a new order.

Yes, the story you're writing has already been told. But no one will tell it the way you will. That's why you write it. ■

Nicole Schroeder

From the Stacks

Courtesy of IndieAuthorTools.com
Got a book you love and want to share with us?
Submit a book at IndieAuthorTools.com

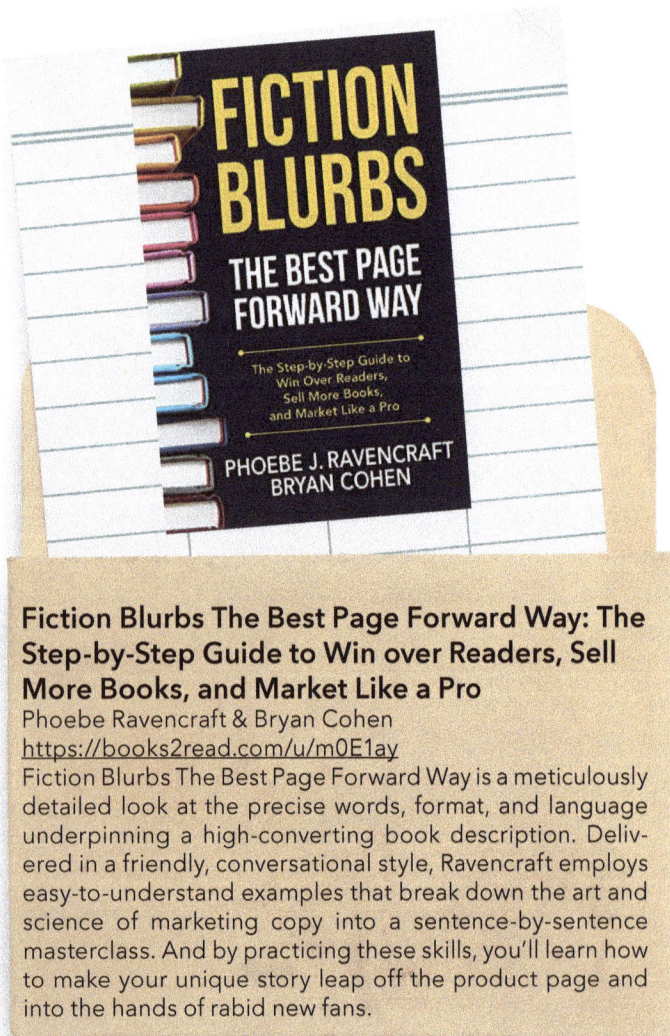

Fiction Blurbs The Best Page Forward Way: The Step-by-Step Guide to Win over Readers, Sell More Books, and Market Like a Pro

Phoebe Ravencraft & Bryan Cohen
https://books2read.com/u/m0E1ay

Fiction Blurbs The Best Page Forward Way is a meticulously detailed look at the precise words, format, and language underpinning a high-converting book description. Delivered in a friendly, conversational style, Ravencraft employs easy-to-understand examples that break down the art and science of marketing copy into a sentence-by-sentence masterclass. And by practicing these skills, you'll learn how to make your unique story leap off the product page and into the hands of rabid new fans.

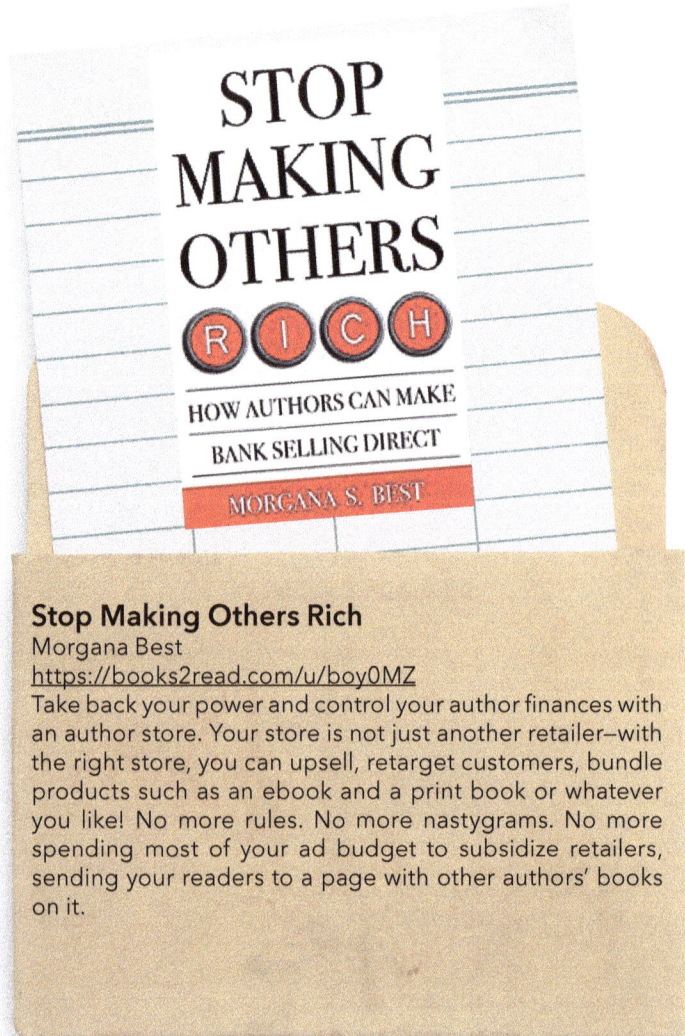

Stop Making Others Rich

Morgana Best
https://books2read.com/u/boy0MZ

Take back your power and control your author finances with an author store. Your store is not just another retailer—with the right store, you can upsell, retarget customers, bundle products such as an ebook and a print book or whatever you like! No more rules. No more nastygrams. No more spending most of your ad budget to subsidize retailers, sending your readers to a page with other authors' books on it.

This book delivers methods that will work for you.
It studies blurbs from a copywriting, neuroscience and artistic perspective.
Because a good blurb is all these things.
This book will dispel blurb myths, and explain effective tactics. Finally, it'll deconstruct great blurbs so you see their moving parts.

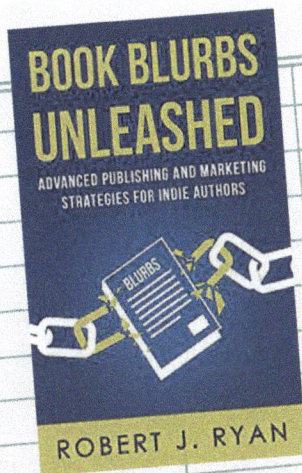

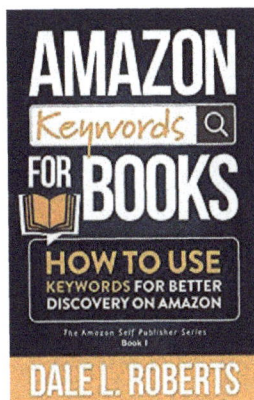

Book Blurbs Unleashed: Advanced Publishing and Marketing Strategies for Indie Authors (Self-publishing Guide 2)

Robert J. Ryan

https://books2read.com/u/mlXQMZ

A blurb is the hub around which all buying decisions revolve. People click to it from the cover. They click to it from ads. They click to it from other books. But how do you write one that turns views into sales?

Do you get conflicting advice on how to write a blurb from books, blogposts and internet comments? Have you tried gimmicks from blurb gurus only to see no difference in sales?

Amazon Keywords for Books: How to Use Keywords for Better Discovery on Amazon

Dale L. Roberts

https://books2read.com/u/3LVJ8w

Key takeaways:

The importance & function of keywords

How to fill the 7 backend keyword slots in KDP

Why keyword relevance determines your success

How to leverage search engines to do your work

The most wonderful part is the AMS Ads tool might be the best kept secret in keyword research and Dale will show you how to get the most out of it.

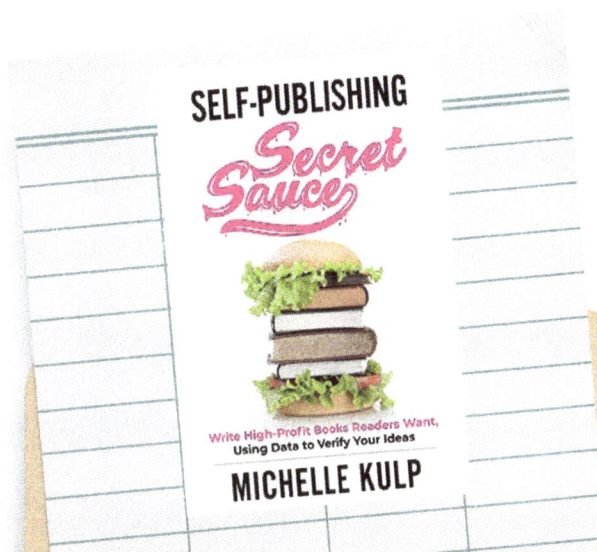

Self-Publishing Secret Sauce: Write High-Profit Books Readers Want, Using Data to Verify Your Ideas

Michelle Kulp

https://books2read.com/u/m2dnJd

Every successful business has a Secret Sauce.

If you want to become a successful self-published author, it's important you learn how to use data to verify your ideas before you write your book.

This will ensure that you have a high-profit topic that readers are actually looking for.

In This Issue

Executive Team

Chelle Honiker, Publisher

As the publisher of Indie Author Magazine, Chelle Honiker brings nearly three decades of startup, technology, training, and executive leadership experience to the role. She's a serial entrepreneur, founding and selling multiple successful companies including a training development company, travel agency, website design and hosting firm, a digital marketing consultancy, and a wedding planning firm. She's organized and curated multiple TEDx events and hired to assist other nonprofit organizations as a fractional executive, including The Travel Institute and The Freelance Association.

As a writer, speaker, and trainer she believes in the power of words and their ability to heal, inspire, incite, and motivate. Her greatest inspiration is her daughters, Kelsea and Cathryn, who tolerate her tendency to run away from home to play with her friends around the world for months at a time. It's said she could run a small country with just the contents of her backpack.

Alice Briggs, Creative Director

As the creative director of Indie Author Magazine, Alice Briggs utilizes her more than three decades of artistic exploration and expression, business startup adventures, and leadership skills. A serial entrepreneur, she has started several successful businesses. She brings her experience in creative direction, magazine layout and design, and graphic design in and outside of the indie author community to her role.

With a masters of science in Occupational Therapy, she has a broad skill set and uses it to assist others in achieving their desired goals. As a writer, teacher, healer, and artist, she loves to see people accomplish all they desire. She's excited to see how IAM will encourage many authors to succeed in whatever way they choose. She hopes to meet many of you in various places around the world once her passport is back in use.

Nicole Schroeder, Editor in Chief

Nicole Schroeder is a storyteller at heart. As the editor in chief of Indie Author Magazine, she brings nearly a decade of journalism and editorial experience to the publication, delighting in any opportunity to tell true stories and help others do the same. She holds a bachelor's degree from the Missouri School of Journalism and minors in English and Spanish. Her previous work includes editorial roles at local publications, and she's helped edit and produce numerous fiction and nonfiction books, including a Holocaust survivor's memoir, alongside independent publishers. Her own creative writing has been published in national literary magazines. When she's not at her writing desk, Nicole is usually in the saddle, cuddling her guinea pigs, or spending time with family. She loves any excuse to talk about Marvel movies and considers National Novel Writing Month its own holiday.

Writers

Gill Fernley

Gill Fernley writes fiction in several genres under different pen names, but what all of them have in common is humour and romance, because she can't resist a happy ending or a good laugh. She's also a freelance content writer and has been running her own business since 2013. Before that, she was a technical author and documentation manager for an engineering company and can describe to you more than you'd ever wish to know about airflow and filtration in downflow booths. Still awake? Wow, that's a first! Anyway, that experience taught her how to explain complex things in straightforward language and she hopes it will come in handy for writing articles for IAM. Outside of writing, she's a cake decorator, expert shoe hoarder, and is fluent in English, dry humour and procrastibaking.

Belinda Griffin

Belinda K Griffin is a Book Marketing Coach and Author Publicity Expert at SmartAuthorsLab.com. She helps authors of all kinds launch and market their books with impact, so they can grow a thriving community of engaged readers and sell more books. Growing a loyal readership and securing publicity through authentic relationship building and outreach is at the heart of everything she teaches.

Chrishaun Keller-Hanna

Chrishaun Keller-Hanna is an award-winning journalist, teacher, technical writer, and fiction author that lives for explaining difficult concepts in a way that non-technical readers can understand.

She spent twenty years teaching literacy and composition to a variety of students from kindergarten to college level and writing technical documentation for several tech companies in the Austin area. At the age of forty-three, she decided to write fiction and has published over thirty titles so far with plans to extend out to comics and board games.

When she's not writing, she's traveling, playing video games, or watching movies. When she's not doing THAT, she's talking about them with her husband and grown daughters.

Megan Linski-Fox

Megan Linski lives in Michigan. She is a USA TODAY Bestselling Author and the author of more than fifty novels. She has over fifteen years of experience writing books alongside working as a journalist and editor. She graduated from the University of Iowa, where she studied Creative Writing.

Megan advocates for the rights of the disabled, and is an activist for mental health awareness. She co-writes the Hidden Legends Universe with Alicia Rades. She also writes under the pen name of Natalie Erin for the Creatures of the Lands series, co-authored by Krisen Lison.

Craig Martelle

High school Valedictorian enlists in the Marine Corps under a guaranteed tank contract. An inauspicious start that was quickly superseded by excelling in language study. Contract waived, a year at the Defense Language Institute to learn Russian and off to keep my ears on the big red machine during the Soviet years. Back to DLI for advanced Russian after reenlisting. Deploying. Then getting selected to get a commission. Earned a four-year degree in two years by majoring in Russian Language. It was a cop out, but I wanted to get back to the fleet. One summa cum laude graduation later, that's where I found myself. My first gig as a second lieutenant was on a general staff. I did well enough that I stayed at that level or higher for the rest of my career, while getting some choice side gigs – UAE, Bahrain, Korea, Russia, and Ukraine.

Major Martelle. I retired from the Marines after a couple years at the embassy in Moscow working arms control issues. The locals called me The German, because of my accent in Russian. That worked for me. It kept me off the radar. Just until it didn't. Expelled after two years for activities inconsistent with my diplomatic status, I went to Ukraine. Can't let twenty years of Russian language go to waste. More arms control. More diplomatic stuff. Then 9/11 and off to war. That was enough deployment for me. Then came retirement.

Department of Homeland Security was a phenomenally miserable gig. I quit that job quickly enough and went to law school. A second summa cum laude later and I was working for a high-end consulting firm performing business diagnostics, business law, and leadership coaching. More deployments. For the money they paid me, I was good with that. Just until I wasn't. Then I started writing. You'll find Easter eggs from my career hidden within all my books. Enjoy the stories.

Angie Martin

Award-winning author Angie Martin has spent over a decade mentoring and helping new and experienced authors as they prepare to send their babies into the world. She relies on her criminal justice background and knack for researching the tiniest of details to assist others when crafting their own novels. She has given countless speeches in various aspects of writing, including creating characters, self-publishing, and writing supernatural and paranormal. She also assisted in leading a popular California writers' group, which organized several book signings for local authors. In addition to having experience in film, she created the first interactive murder mystery on Clubhouse and writes and directs each episode. Angie now resides in rural Tennessee, where she continues to help authors around the world in every stage of publication while writing her own thriller and horror books, as well as branching out into new genres.

Merri Maywether

Merri Maywether lives with her husband in rural Montana. You can find her in the town's only coffee house listening to three generations of Montanans share their stories. Otherwise, she's in the classroom or the school library, inspiring the next generation's writers.

Susan Odev

Susan has banked over three decades of work experience in the fields of personal and organizational development, being a freelance corporate trainer and consultant alongside holding down "real" jobs for over twenty-five years. Specializing in entrepreneurial mindsets, she has written several non-fiction business books, once gaining a coveted Amazon #1 best seller tag in business and entrepreneurship, an accolade she now strives to emulate with her fiction.

Currently working on her fifth novel, under a top secret pen name, the craft and marketing aspects of being a successful indie author equally fascinate and terrify her.

A lover of history with a criminal record collection, Susan lives in a retro orange and avocado world. Once described by a colleague as being an "onion," Susan has many layers, as have ogres (according to Shrek). She would like to think this makes her cool, her teenage children just think she's embarrassing.

MERCH FOR AUTHORS

Branded merch on Etsy, Amazon, and your own site.
Learn about extended stock licenses.
Includes sample contracts.

envato elements

Travel & Hotel Email Builder
By theemon

Travel Email Builder
By HyperPix

Kant - Email Template
By ThemeMountain

Olive - Fashion Email Template
By giantdesign

Metro App - Instapage Template
By Morad

ButaPest Email Template
By JeetuG

All the Email Templates you need and many other design elements, are available for a monthly subscription by subscribing to Envato Elements. The subscription costs $16.50 per month and gives you **unlimited access** to a massive and growing library of **1,500,000+** items that can be downloaded as often as you need (stock photos too)!

DOWNLOAD NOW

COME VISIT

the *Cake Machine* STAY for the *Conference.*

Las Vegas
Nevada
November
14-18, 2022

writelink.to/20Books

20 BOOKS
TO 50K®
A RISING TIDE LIFTS ALL BOATS

www.ingramcontent.com/pod-product-compliance
Lightning Source LLC
Chambersburg PA
CBHW052344210326
41597CB00037B/6254